TOWARDS A
NEW THEATRE

TOWARDS A
NEW THEATRE

The Lectures of
ROBERT EDMOND JONES

Transcribed and edited with
an introduction and commentary by
DELBERT UNRUH

Limelight Editions

First Limelight Edition March 1992

Copyright © 1992 by Delbert Unruh

We are grateful to the heirs of Prof. Frederick C. Packard, who gave us permission to publish transcripts of the Jones lectures he recorded.

"The New Theatre of Robert Edmond Jones" reprinted from TD&T with permission of the United States Institute for Theatre Technology, Inc.

Illustrative material courtesy of University Archives, Swem Library, College of William and Mary.

Library of Congress Cataloging-in-Publication Data
Jones, Robert Edmond, 1887–1954.
    Towards a new theatre : the lectures of Robert Edmond Jones / transcribed and edited with an introduction and commentary by Delbert Unruh.—1st Limelight ed.
        p.   cm.
    Includes bibliographical references.
    ISBN 0–87910–152–0
    1. Motion pictures and theater.   2. Theater—United States.
I. Unruh, Delbert.   II. Title.
PN1995.25.J6   1992
792'.0973—dc20   91–37925
                                                          CIP

TABLE OF CONTENTS

DEDICATION

Beginning sometime around 1941, Robert Edmond Jones made himself available for public lecture tours. During the following years, Jones traveled throughout the United States speaking at colleges and universities and other gatherings of organizations concerned with the future of the arts in America.

In May, 1952, at the invitation of Professor Frederick C. Packard Jr., Robert Edmond Jones came to Harvard University to record his lectures. Following Jones's death in 1955, Professor Packard released the first two of the lectures in the form of a long-playing record. Later on in 1963, Professor Packard released the remaining two lectures in the form of a reel-to-reel tape. On the jacket of the first recording, Professor Packard noted, in part, the following.

> The mortal voice of America's foremost theatre artist is stilled, but his impact on the American Theatre remains . . .
>
> The American theatre has been permanently enriched and ennobled by the contagious excitement of his stimulating spirit. He toured the country to share his ideals with theatre-minded youth, urging them to reject tawdry realism, slick emptiness, Broadway show business, and challenging them to embrace his dream of a revitalized theatre holding to lofty ideals . . .
>
> Dates, facts, statistics about R. E. Jones can be ascertained in reference libraries and theatre libraries and theatre collections, but THE fact about him was his missionary zeal for the theatre—his ability to infect everyone he met with a sense of the glory, excitement, and deep satisfaction of a life dedicated to the highest ideals of art . . .

How to make the theatre a living art—a pulsing true reflection of the incessantly changing drama of our time—that was Jones's dream. No one could have lived that dream more fully nor have shared it more generously than did Robert Edmond Jones.

The foresight and dedication of Prof. Packard insured that these lectures were preserved, and it is to his memory that this book is respectfully dedicated.

DELBERT UNRUH
Lawrence, Kansas
April, 1991

ACKNOWLEDGMENTS

I would like to thank the following people who have helped me immeasurably in the research, preparation, and completion of this project.

During the research phase, many librarians, archivists, and individuals contributed to this project. They include: the staff of the Library of Congress; Sharron G. Uhler, Archivist at the University of Missouri, Kansas City; Lowell W. Coolidge of the Andrews Library at the College of Wooster, Wooster, Ohio; James W. Oberly of the Earl Gregg Swem Library at the College of William and Mary, Williamsburg, Virginia; Lois Hendrickson at the Walter Library at the University of Minnesota; Jeanne Newill at the Harvard Theatre Collection; Stephen C. Jones of the Bienecke Library at Yale University; and especially Professor Horace W. Robinson, Emeritus Professor of Theatre at the University of Oregon, who graciously shared his recollections of Jones's visit to his campus in 1949.

During the preparation of this book, two people performed an extraordinary service in the transcription of the tapes and the editing of the manuscript. My wife, Ione, and our dear friend from South Africa, Joanne Van Rensberg, spent countless hours, along with me, listening to and transcribing the tapes and then re-listening to the tapes and editing the transcripts. They have my love and thanks. During the book's final stages, Peter Packard, John Packard, and Penelope Strand, the children of Professor Frederick C. Packard and his wife Alice, welcomed my contacts and inquiries concerning their father's work and attendant copyright questions. They permitted and encouraged me to bring this project to completion. I am in their debt for their indispensable help and encouragement. More important, however, is the fact that all who read this book are in debt to their father who had the foresight and dedication to record the lectures at Harvard in 1952.

Finally, any author, or editor/author in my case, must make acknowledgement of the sources of inspiration, insofar as that is possible. In my case it is quite easy. It was Professor Sam Ball at Northwestern University who introduced me to the first two Jones lectures in 1964. He also knew, because of his study with Donald Oenslager at Yale University, that there were two more lectures that had never been released. Great teachers have a way of planting seeds in the minds of their students without knowing when or if they will ever germinate, grow, and flower. This book is one of the flowers, Sam, and I thank you for its seed.

Part One

Introduction and Commentary

Introduction

The lectures of Robert Edmond Jones are a forgotten treasure of the American Theatre. This complete aesthetic statement on the nature and future of the theatre by America's foremost stage designer is almost completely unknown today, even though the four lectures, collectively known as *Towards A New Theatre*, spelled out Jones's personal vision of the American theatre as it was and as it ought to be. They are passionate attempts to alter the development of an American theatre that Jones saw as being stuck in a retrograde and backward position. His vision of a "New Theatre" was comprehensive and his perceptions challenged the playwrights, directors, actors, producers, and designers of his day. They will challenge the artists of today's theatre when they are known again.

We have no way of knowing precisely when Jones developed the four lectures, but we do know certain things about their evolution and dissemination. We know, for example, that on January 14, 1941, Jones entered into arrangements with the Lee Keedick Agency for a series of lecture tours.[1] Promotional literature from the Keedick agency circa 1948 (frontispiece and Figures 1, 2, and 3) states that at that time Jones was prepared to speak on three topics: "The Theatre Of The Future," "The Art Of The Theatre," and "Why We Have Theatres." We know that following his agreement with Keedick, Jones visited many colleges and universities during the next few years.[2]

We also know, however, that during this time Jones did not restrict his appearances to campuses. A typed manuscript edited in Jones's own hand of a lecture entitled "The Drama Of The Future" exists from a presentation that Jones gave at the Drama Symposium held at the Metropolitan Museum of Art on January 21, 1943. This lecture differs only in title, introduction, and topical allusions from the Harvard recording of the lecture identified in the Keedick promotional material as "The Theatre Of The Future." Apparently Jones changed the title and introduction in order to make the lecture fit the needs of the museum event.

In 1952 we know that Jones delivered his four lectures at Harvard University under the general title *Towards A New Theatre*. The lectures were recorded by Professor Frederick C. Packard and two of them, "The Theatre Of The Future" and "The Art Of The Theatre," were released under that general title by Professor Packard as a limited edition Vocarium Record in November, 1955, following Jones's death on November 26, 1954.[3] It is in this form that they are known, if at all, today. The limited edition of the recording and the inevitable small market for it assured that the lectures had a restricted circulation. The passage of time only further eroded knowledge of the recording. In 1963 Vocarium Records released the other two lectures in the form of a 7½ IPS 2-track reel-to-reel tape. One of these seems to be the third of the lectures advertised by the Keedick Agency, "Why We Have Theatres." The other lecture on the tape, "Curious And Profitable," had been privately printed as a pamphlet and circulated by Jones sometime earlier.[4] The marketing of this recording seems to have been even more selective than the first, and America's headlong rush into the late 60's and its preoccupation with Viet-nam and social and cultural change resulted in an even smaller circulation for it. Jones didn't seem to have much to say to that age—or circumstances, at least, made sure that the age didn't hear his voice.

So, by the end of the 60's, it is fair to say, the Jones lectures were, for the most part, completely forgotten. Jones's legacy to the American Theatre was thus reduced, essentially, to three books: *Drawings For The Theater*, published in 1925, *The Dramatic Imagination*, published in 1941, and *The Theatre Of Robert Edmond Jones*, edited by Ralph Pendleton and published in 1958. While all of them advanced the thoughts of Jones, the "last testament" of the lectures was now in limbo.

I first became aware of the lectures in 1965. I was then a graduate student at Northwestern University and Sam Ball, the design professor, routinely played the Vocarium recording of the first two lectures for the design classes. I was, of course, aware of the Jones's books, which were a staple of theatre eduction at that time. In fact, *The Dramatic Imagination* was then a bible for students in the theatre. But it was an extraordinary experience to hear the recordings and to be "in Jones's presence," so to speak. Even so, my own interest in the lectures waned during the late 60's in the climate and under the pressures of the time. Sometime later, in 1977, I found myself at the University of Kansas as the head of the design program and as the instructor in an undergraduate class called "Approaching Design For The Theatre." The catalog description of this course was sufficiently opaque so as to disguise its content and I knew, at that point, that I was not interested in teaching a class on systems of artificial perspective and the mysteries of the scale ruler. A course that combined the aesthetics and history of design seemed more to my liking, and as I developed and organized the content of the course the Jones lectures came immediately to mind. A trip to Evanston to visit Sam yielded a cassette of the recording, which was to prove the centerpiece of the content of the course—the centerpiece because a curious thing happened when I played the recording for my class in 1978. At the end of the lecture "The Art Of The Theatre,"

A SCENE FROM *GREEN PASTURES*
(Courtesy of Farrar & Reinhardt)
DESIGNED BY ROBERT EDMOND JONES

LECTURE SUBJECTS:

THE THEATRE OF THE FUTURE

THE ART OF THE THEATRE

WHY WE HAVE THEATRES

Figure 1

which I always played first; the following exchange took place. It has been repeated in one variation or another in every class ever since.

"When did he record these lectures?"
"1952."
"Funny, I thought he was talking about our theatre today."

The repetition of that exchange, every fall for several years, convinced me that my sense of the worth of Jones's lectures was more than just personal or antiquarian. Accordingly, I began an informal, sporadic, but persistent survey, asking colleagues in design and theatre, wherever and whenever I encountered them, if they had ever heard the Jones lectures. To my amazement, at least 99 percent said no. Further, most were not even aware that the lectures existed or were accessible. My interest grew with every response and with the annual playing of the first Vocarium recording. In 1983 I began a more systematic investigation of the lectures by searching out records of Jones's lecture tour and copies of the remaining two lectures. After many false starts, blind alleys, and blunt inquires, and with the generous assistance of many librarians, archivists, and friends, I at last acquired the recording of lectures 3 and 4 and various items of supporting material. What had started out as a search motivated by simple curiosity became a quest and, once I was in possession of all four lectures, an obsession. This book is the result of that obsession. These lectures are as relevant to our theatre today as they were in 1952. It is profitable to hear them.

ROBERT EDMOND JONES

THE influence of the personality of Robert Edmond Jones in the contemporary theatre has become a contemporary legend. For more than two decades he has been a pioneer—blazing a path which has profoundly affected the whole of modern theatre design. To audiences who have sat rapt before his impressive work he is essentially a poet, a master of light and color, the creator of the imagined lands in which a pillar rising to the sky in "THE JEST" is the image of the late Renaissance, or a guttering candle in a dark room becomes the Russia of "REDEMPTION." In his career in the theatre he has desiged such historic productions as "THE MAN WHO MARRIED A DUMB WIFE," John Barrymore's "RICHARD THE THIRD" and "HAMLET," Lionel Barrymore's "MACBETH," "ROADSIDE," most of Eugene O'Neill's plays, the tender and moving "GREEN PASTURES" and many others. All of which have brought him recognition as the greatest designer the American theatre has produced.

He has done much besides designing for the stage, however. He is also a director, and is responsible for the remarkable productions which have been given at the Central City Opera House in Colorado. When the movies first began their experiments with color, it was Robert Edmond Jones who was called in by RKO to stage the revolutionary color picture "LA CUCARACHA" as well as "BECKY SHARP."

Today Robert Edmond Jones stands at the pinnacle of his career in the American theatre. But always, he is the pioneer, looking forward toward the theatre of tomorrow. In his lecture he presents such profound truths of the theatre, stated with such clarity, with such a wealth of allusion and anecdote that one does not at first realize their profundity. Moreover with compelling logic and skill, Robert Edmond Jones challenges convention in his forecasts of a theatre of tomorrow in which motion pictures and radio will play so large a part.

He brings to the platform a wealth of experience, a keen penetrating mind and a charming personality that have made him a platform favorite wherever he has appeared.

Mr. Jones is the recipient of the Howland Memorial Prize presented at Yale University in 1926 and the Fine Arts Medal presented by the American Institute of Architects for conspicuous attainment as a designed of the theatre. He is also the author with Kenneth McGowan of "CONTINENTAL STAGECRAFT," and the forthcoming "THE DRAMATIC IMAGINATION."

Figure 2

PROFILE

From An Article by Gilbert Seldes in the New Yorker

★　　★

IN a profession notorious for its quick intimacies, in a period of self-exploitation and ballyhoo, Robert Edmond Jones, a master of the theatre and a man profoundly at home in his age, has chosen to live quietly. At a time when the commercial stage was becoming harder and slicker and ever flashier, he brought to it powerful impulses of an austere and poetical purity; and to the art theatre he brought a practical mastery, a willingness to work with the existing material, a discipline and control. At the Bergman Studio, where the technique of scene-painting has been marvelously developed in the past decade, Jones is known as a master of light and color, a craftsman as well as an artist, and is held in high esteem because his dimensions are always right, because his sketches always come in on time, because he provides a hundred diagrams in various scales, if necessary, to make the work of the painters easier.

What distinguishes his work is a combination of vigor with taste. Or, I should have put it this way: that any of his virtues taken singly might produce an unbalanced artist, or a priggish one, or even a pedantic one, or a mad one, and the important thing is that he combines things which correct each other without letting one corrupt the other. He creates, and as his lectures and writing show, is perfectly able to explain what he has created..

As someone has said: "What happens to Jones is ultimately what happens to the American theatre."

Exclusive Management:

LEE KEEDICK, 475 Fifth Avenue, New York, N. Y.

Figure 3

Commentary

A general note: The numbering of the lectures that I have used herein is to a certain extent arbitrary. Its only claim to legitimacy is that it follows the listing of the three lectures in the promotional brochure from the Keedick Agency.

LECTURE NO. 1—*The Theatre of the Future*

I believe that this lecture is the centerpiece of the set. It is the one that contains, in the clearest possible terms, Jones's vision of a "New Theatre"—the fusion of theatre and motion pictures. The idea of this fusion had occupied Jones for many years. As early as 1929 he set out his vision in the *Encyclopedia Britannica.* He continued to work on it in other writings from that time on. An abbreviated version of it appeared in *The Dramatic Imagination* in 1941, and the rich and varied idea of a synthesis of film and theatre continued to engage his mind until the time of his death. He could reshape the lecture and his thoughts to suit a specific audience, as he did with the speech, "The Drama Of The Future," that he delivered to the Drama Symposium at the Metropolitan Museum in 1943; and he could take a different tack on the problem as he did in "Curious And Profitable," the fourth lecture in this set. But in any guise, and in any form, this idea—the fusion of film and live theatre—is central to the thoughts of Jones, and it is a vision that had taken the American theatre a long time to absorb. Jones's ideas were far in advance of his audiences' ability to comprehend. It is only now that we see experiments that begin to validate Jones's vision. The idea is more pertinent today than it was in 1929, or 1941, or 1943, or 1952, or 1963. A close reading of it will reveal fantastic possibilities for a theatre that is just now beginning to emerge.

LECTURE NO. 2—*The Art of the Theatre*

This lecture is a "feel good lecture." I suspect it is the one Jones used for audiences who might not be that well-versed in the theatre. This lecture shows Jones at his poetic, romantic best; exhorting workers in the theatre to dream, to imagine and to: "let the dynamis of the true artist enter into you. Take the little gift you have into the hall of the gods." This is heady stuff. Poetic, inspirational, romantic, and awe-inspiring—this is the Jones of *The Dramatic Imagination*.

LECTURE NO. 3—*Why We Have Theatres*

This, the first lecture on the tape released by Vocarium Records in 1963 and now, almost totally unknown, is a radical departure from the conventional image we have of Jones. This is not the Jones of *The Dramatic Imagination*. This is the confrontational Jones. This is Jones delivering a blunt, straightforward, unvarnished assessment of the American theatre and the workers in it. There are some parallels to Lecture No. 2 and some passages from that lecture are incorporated into this one but the tone is different. Jones is issuing a challenge and he pulls no punches:

The essential American soul is hard, isolate, stoic, and a
killer. It has never been melted.

and:

> ... I want you to get a sense of responsibility towards the
> theatre. And then I want you to throw out the trash—the
> trash in the theatre and the trash in your own thinking.

and:

> We must not make the mistake of blaming the movies, or
> the radio, or television for the decline of the theatre. We
> must blame the theatre for the decline of the theatre. It
> has not been destroyed by hostile outside influences. It
> has rotted away from within.

and:

> Someday an audience is going to rise to its feet, en masse,
> during a performance and say, "Who do you think we
> are? What kind of people do you take us for?" I hope I
> am in the theatre that night.

This lecture gives us an insight into the revolutionary that
Jones was first and foremost. This lecture is direct. It is a
challenge. It is a slap in the face.

Lecture No. 4—*Curious and Profitable*

This was not one of the lectures advertised in the Keedick
promotional literature. It seems that Jones wrote it sometime
before 1941 and then printed it himself and privately circulated
it. The lecture takes the form of an extended conversation

between Jones and an imaginary visitor he has conjured up for purposes of examining the state of the American theatre. Two things are of note here, I believe. One, Jones uses the imaginary construct of the essay as a device for expanding his ideas of the "New Theatre"—the fusion of film and theatre. The essay, then, is in the mainline of Jones's thinking and is another of the many writings and presentations that he made in developing the vision of his new theatre. Second, a persistent theme in all the lectures is Jones's insistence that the theatre is out of touch with its time and is operating with outworn conventions. In Lecture 4 he returns to that theme with a sense of urgency. And it is this urgency when heard today in the world of today—with the end of the cold war, the growing awareness of a potential environmental catastrophe, and the demonstrated impotence of all political systems in the face of major social issues—that gives the following quote a special contemporary relevance:

> We are in the midst of a bewildering breakdown of outworn conventions and a slow and painful growth of new ones. The world is moving, in agony, toward a new consciousness. But for some reason your theatre reflects little of this tension—the horrifying unawareness of life in the face of the drama that is being played out on the front page of every newspaper.

It is that sense—the sense that Jones is talking about today—that conditions the response that emerges in my class every year. It is that sense that identifies the worth of these lectures. And it is also that sense that lets us know how far we have to travel even to approach a new theatre.

Part Two

The Lectures

Lecture 1

The Theatre of the Future

L adies and Gentlemen. A drama is not a picture. It is not a symphony. It is not a lecture or a sermon. It is a "show" of life, lived out in our presence. Acted out by players who, "hold as 'twere the mirror up to Nature—".[1] As we are in life so the theatre is. And as life moves and changes so the theatre moves and changes with it. Now life is changing with such rapidity that we can hardly keep pace with it from one moment to the next. We are shot through the stratosphere in jet planes at supersonic speeds. We write in the sky in letters of smoke to advertise the latest popular beverage. We appear at the same instant on a thousand television screens. "Hepcats" swing and sway in jam-sessions. The wife of a fashionable surrealist painter adorns her hat with a raw pork chop on the occasion of the opening of her husband's most recent exhibition. How shall we withstand these tastes and pressures of the world? Is it any wonder that, in the words of the poet Yeats, "our rhythm shudders"? Such happenings, however, are symptoms, not causes, of change. The real change is the deeper one—is the change in our consciousness. A new awareness is in the world—something which was not there before. I believe that this new awareness, this new approach to life, will influence the theatre very greatly in the near future. Before long—shall we say in five years, ten years, a quarter of a century; the actual time does not matter—a radically new kind of theatre will have taken shape. Can we get an inkling of what this new theatre will be like? I think we can.

Let us look backward for a moment before we begin to look forward. With your permission I will read you certain excerpts from several well known dramas of the past. We call them classics. My purpose is to evoke in your minds the characteristic qualities of various epochs in the theatre's history—their atmosphere, their special flavor. The first is a passage from the *Antigone* of Sophocles:

> Wonders are many, and none is more wonderful than man; . . . the power that crosses the white sea driven by the south-wind, making a path under the surges that threaten to engulf him; and Earth, the eldest of the gods, the immortal, the unwearied doth he wear as a garment . . .
>
> .   .   .   .
>
> And speech, and wind-swift thought; and all the words that mould a state, hath he taught himself, and how to flee the arrows of the frost, when 'tis hard lodging under the clear sky . . . yea, he hath resource for all but death . . . against death shall he call for aid in vain:

Here is a fragment from a drama of the Middle Ages. You will recognize it at once:

> I pray you all give your audience,
> And hear this matter with reverence,
> By figure a moral play—

The *Summoning of Everyman* called it is,
That of our lives and ending shows
How transitory we be all day.
.   .   .   .

The story saith,—Man, in the beginning
Look well, and give good heed to the ending.
Be you never so gay!

Now a scene from another kind of drama. Romeo has come to
the great ball at the house of Capulet. He is wearing the white
robe of a pilgrim. He is face-to-face with Juliet for the first
time. He takes her hand:

If I profane with my unworthiest hand
This holy shrine, the gentle fine is this
My lips, two blushing pilgrims, ready stand
To smooth that rough touch with a tender kiss.

Good pilgrim, you do wrong your hand too much,
Which mannerly devotion shows in this;
That saints have hands which pilgrims love to touch,
And palm to palm is holy palmers' kiss.

Have not saints lips, and holy palmers too?

Aye, pilgrim, lips that they must use in prayer.

Why then, dear saint, let lips do what hands do.

And here is a snatch of dialogue from still another kind of
drama. William Congreve set it down in 1700(2):

But, dear Millamant, why were you so long?

Long! Lord, have I not made violent haste; I have asked
every living thing I met for you: I have inquired after
you as after a new fashion.

.   .   .   .

You were dressed before I came abroad.

Ay, that's true—O but then I had—Let me see, what had I?
Why was I so long?
Oh men, your la'ship stayed to peruse a packet of letters.

> . . . —I hate letters—Nobody knows how to write letters,
> and yet one has 'em, one does not know why. They serve
> to pin up one's hair.

> Is that the way? Pray, madam, do you pin up your hair
> with all your letters? I find I must keep copies.

> Only with those in verse, Master Witwell, I never pin up
> my hair with prose.

Now let us jump across the centuries down to a Broadway
success of several seasons ago, *The Man Who Came To Dinner*[3]:

> . . . What are you giving me for Christmas, Jefferson? I
> have enriched your feeble life beyond your capacity to
> repay me.

> Yes, that's what I figured, so I'm not giving you anything.

> I see. Well, I was giving you my old truss, but now I
> shan't.

Now I quote from another popular success, *The Women*[4]:

> . . . Lucy, were you ever in love?

> Yes, ma'am.

> Tell me about it, Lucy.

> Well, ma'am, ain't much to tell. I was kinda enjoyn' the
> courtin' time. It was as purty a sight as you ever saw, to

see him come lopin' across them hills. The sky so big and blue and that hair of his, blazing like the be-jesuss in the sun. Then we'd sit on my back fence and spark. But, ma'am, you know how them big, strong, red-headed men are. They just got to get to the point. So we got married, ma'am. And natcheraly, I ain't had no chanct to think about love since—

In citing these various examples of drama I have no intention of comparing them one with another. As Mrs. Malaprop reminds us, "Caparisons are odorous." The point I am making is: That the last two plays, I have chosen them almost at random, are nothing more or less than candid-camera shots presented in terms of the theatre. And they are related to the dramas of the past in precisely the same way that the excellent photographs reproduced weekly in our popular magazines are related to the vase paintings of the Greek artist Douris, or to the mosaics in Ravenna, or to the allegorical canvasses of Titian, or Veronese, or to the great English portraits of the eighteenth century. To compare them with the classics of the theatre would be like comparing a banquet to a concert. The point is this. Neither of the last two dramas would have been written in the way it was written if it had not been for the invention of the camera.

The growth of realism in the theatre during the latter half of the nineteenth century and the beginning of the twentieth is a commonplace of theatrical history. But it is not possible for us to form a complete picture of the realistic drama, or the realistic theatre, without taking into consideration the photographic habit of mind which has been implanted in us more and more deeply as the mechanism for taking photographs has been developed and perfected through the years. The first photograph was lifted from its bath of chemicals only a little over a century ago. In this short space of time, as time is reckoned, the camera has utterly changed the quality of our perception. For better or for worse, we have all become "camera-minded". For a time, during the early years of the twentieth century, it seemed that the theatre was becoming preoccupied with the sheer surface of things, to an alarming extent. Insight dwindled into mere reporting. Our dreary averageness was publicized and glorified. Many of us remember, with embarrassment, the Childs Restaurant transferred bodily to the stage of the Belasco Theatre in the third act of *The Governor's Lady*. Complete: with *real* coffee urns, and *real* waiters—yes, and *real* buttercakes. I saw them! I was there!

But at the same time, other influences had been at work— leavening influences. While the majority of our writers were busy applying the "common sense" method of approach to literature in general and to the theatre in particular; Henrik Ibsen had already written of a lady who suffered from a curious malady—an obsession—an unexplainable longing for the sea. What a magical, troubling play that was! And what new vistas of thought it opened out to us[5]:

. . . Go with him! Place your fate in his hands!

Could I not place my fate in your hands?

.   .   .   .

At least you knew what kind of life you were entering upon . . . But what do you know now? . . . not even who he is or what he is.

That is true. But that is just the terrible thing.

Yes, terrible indeed——

And that is why I feel as if I must give way to it.

Because it seems terrible to you?

Yes, . . .

Tell me Ellida—what do you really mean by "terrible"?

I call a thing terrible—when it both frightens and fascinates me.

Fascinates?

Most of all when it fascinates me— . . .

You were akin to the sea.

There is terror in that too.

And Maurice Maeterlinck was dreaming of vast inscrutable destinies, and dark ancestral forests—by the light of day never entered—and ancient ruined castles where strange, beautiful, wraith-like women lay dying[6]:

Open the window . . . open the window . . .

Shall I open this one, Melisanda?

No, no, the great window . . . so I can see . . .

.   .   .   .

Thank you . . . Is it sunset?

Yes; the sun is setting on the sea; it is late. How do you feel, Melisanda?

Well, well . . . . And yet it seems to me that I know something . . .

What are you saying? I do not understand you . . .

I no longer understand all I say . . . I do not know what I am saying . . . I do not know what I know . . .

And William Butler Yeats began to tell of shadowy waters and of a mystical land of heart's desire echoing with the dreamy chanting of the voices of the ever-young[7]:

. . . The world drops away,
And I am left alone with my beloved,
Who cannot put me from his heart for ever.
.   .   .   .

O flower of the branch, O bird among the leaves,
O silver fish that my two hands have taken
Out of the running stream, O morning star,
.   .   .   .

Bend lower, that I may cover you with my hair,
For we will gaze upon this world no longer.

Meanwhile, Henry James was writing his novels in a new and disturbing literary idiom. A style of vague suggestions and delicate intimations—recondite, subtle, inward. Writing as if from another state of consciousness. Here is a paragraph from *The Sense Of The Past:*

It was furthermore of moment that not a shade of disadvantage, even while the impression was suddenest and sharpest, appeared attachable by Ralph's fancy to Sir Cantopher's similar exercise, for how could one in that case have been so moved more and more to advance in proportion as it was suggested that one was awaited?

Then all at once with one bound, so to speak, James Joyce moved boldly into this new region of the consciousness and wrote straight out of the heart of it; making mental montages, in the manner of[8]:

Eglintoneyes, . . . ,looked up shybrightly.

Surely a montage if ever there was one. Or compressing a thousand heartbreaking reveries into the closing lines of *Finnegans Wake:*

. . . Lps. The keys to. Given! A way a lone a last a loved a long the

Here is a passage from *Ulysses:*

Through the hush of air a voice sang to them, low, not rain, not leaves in murmur, like no voice of strings or reeds or whatdoyoucallthem dulcimers, touching their still ears with words, still hearts of their each his remembered lives. Good, good to hear:

  Love that is singing: love's old sweet song.

    —Co-me, thou lost one!
    Co-me thou dear one!
Alone. One love. One hope. One comfort me. Martha, chestnote, return.
    —Come!
It soared, a bird, it held its flight, a swift pure cry, soar silver orb it leaped serene, speeding, sustained, to come, don't spin it out too long long breath he breath long life soaring high, high resplendent, aflame, crowned, high in the effulgence, symbolistic, high of the ethereal bosom, high, of the high vast irradiation everywhere all soaring all around about the all, the endlessnessnessness . . .
    —To me!

  Come. Well sung. All clapped. She ought to. Come. To me, to him, to her, you too, me, us.
    —Bravo!

And now we are face to face with a new kind of literary expression that is not so much expression as "pre-expression"—a thinking aloud, a feeling aloud—thought and emotion caught and held at the instant of its passing from the subjective to the objective—the thought before the utterance.

Many of us still find this kind of writing disturbing, confusing, controversial, even outrageous. But one thing is certain. It is not a deliberately cryptic way of expressing familiar ideas. The ideas, themselves, are new. The new way of writing springs directly from a new way of thinking and feeling. It is an adventure into the world of the mind.

I might liken this adventure to a commando raid. Certain of our modern writers, with Joyce in the vanguard, have set out to explore the vast, shadowy, inner region of the self which we have learned to call the subconscious. They have landed a "token-force", so to speak, on its shores. They have learned something—a little, not much, but something—of its topography, its configuration, and something of its nature and its laws. And they have learned that its language, its Esperanto, its Basic English, shall we say—for the language of the subconscious is a universal one—is a language of images—the images that move and speak in the depths of the self, the dynamic images of our dreams.

It is this new, this other, language that our writers are struggling to perfect. But when we look carefully at their work a strange thing becomes apparent. The further their technique is developed the closer it approaches the technique of the motion picture. Rightly understood, and rightly used, the motion picture is the new language of images they are seeking.

While literature, and painting, and music have been changing; photography has been changing too. We have always liked photographs—these replicas of ourselves and the world about us. In fact, we have liked them so much, we have focused such a burning intensity of interest upon them; that they have begun to move, and speak, and to take on all the colors of life. But here is a curious thing. The moment photographs began to move, they ceased to be a reproduction of our outward experience, and became a projection of our inward experience. I cannot pretend to explain this fact any more than I can explain gravitation. I can only testify to it. It simply is so. We are all making a great mistake in the way we think about motion pictures. They seem so natural, especially now that they have begun to talk and to take on all the colors of life, that we think they are real. But they are not real at all, in the sense in which a still photograph *is* real. A photograph is a picture. But a motion picture is an image. A photograph is tangible—as tangible as a painting hung on a wall. A motion picture, I mean the thing we see at the Tivoli or the Uptown, is intangible. A photograph is objective. A motion picture is subjective—disembodied, evanescent—appearing out of nothingness, vanishing into nothingness, a thought, a memory, a dream—remembered afterward only as dreams are remembered. Up there on the silver screen we see, not ourselves, but our shadow selves. These shifting shadows—flashing from image to image, from sequence to sequence—are our thoughts, our emotions, our desires, our dreams made visible and audible.

Let me illustrate. Here is an auditorium. Here are spectators. Here is a lecturer. These are the outward facts that make up the objective occasion. But while I am talking, and while you are listening, something else is happening. We are all thinking, and we are thinking in a series of images. It is precisely as if a tiny motion picture screen had been installed in the brain of every one of us at birth. On this screen mental images are projected in a never-ending stream from the cradle to the grave. The analogy is apt. That is what thinking is. The motion picture parallels our thought process. The images move as our thoughts do, and like our thoughts, they are free from the limitations of space and time. That is why the movies have such a hypnotic power over us, and that is why they are so dangerous when we confuse them with actuality. A theatre audience is wide awake—united in an active participation in the dramatic excitement of the play. But everyone in a movie audience is alone—pathetically alone—absorbed in his own daydream. If you do not believe it, leave a performance at a theatre in the middle of an act and go quickly to the nearest motion picture theatre and see the difference for yourself. In hundreds of thousands of motion pictures all over the world millions of people are sitting at this very moment—dreaming, dreaming. What new dramatist will awaken us from that dream?

The day we become aware of the fact that a motion picture is a purely mental experience, as a symphony by Beethoven is a mental experience; the day we cease to say, "I saw Joan Fontaine last night."; and realize that what we saw was *not* Joan Fontaine at all but a magical and literally enchanting memory of her; on that day the new language of images will be ours to use in the service of the new drama.

Now, I'm not implying that the drama of tomorrow, or the day after tomorrow, will be a motion picture—far from it. The change I foresee is a far more radical one. I'm exceedingly anxious to be clear on this point. Our experience, the thing that makes us quick and not dead, is neither exclusively objective nor exclusively subjective but *both* objective and subjective. We lead two lives at the same time—a conscious life and a life of the subconscious. We live, and move, and have our being in two worlds—the outer world and the inner world. And the drama which will portray our essential duality will reveal our two natures—the outer and the inner, the seen and the unseen—in a new synthesis.

We shall not find many suggestions of this new synthesis in our playhouses in this year of our Lord 1952. But dramatic literature is crowded with them. Here is one from *Fashion*, a comedy of manners written a hundred years ago. Mrs. Tiffany, an impressionable society matron of New York, is entertaining a bogus count at one of her fashionable receptions[9]:

... I presume you are home in all the courts of Europe, Count?

... yes Madam, ... I believe I am at home in all the courts
of Europe—*police courts.* (Aside, crossing.)

Another example: In 1915, Miss Alice Gerstenberg wrote a
one-act comedy: *Overtones.* The play has only two characters,
both of them women. But each of these characters has two
selves: one of them cultured, exterior; the other primitive,
inner. On a stage the play is acted by four women. I will read
you the concluding speeches. The primitive selves rage at each
other:

I love him—I love him—

He's starving—I'm starving—

.   .   .   .

I want your money—and your influence.

I'm going to rob you—rob you.

The cultured selves say their polite farewells:

I've had such a delightful afternoon.

It has been a joy to see you.

Good-bye.

Good-bye, my dear.

And now I will give you a fragment of a scene from a great
contemporary play, *Strange Interlude*, by Eugene O'Neill.
Nina speaks:

Sit down, all of you! Make yourselves at home!
You are my three men! This is your home with me!
Ssshh! I thought I heard the baby. You must all
sit down and be very quiet. You must not wake our baby.

Now she is thinking aloud:

My three men! . . . I feel their desires converge
in me! . . . they dissolve in me, their life is my life . . .
.   .   .   .
Why, I should be the proudest woman on earth! . . .
I should be the happiest woman in the world! . . .
only I better knock wood . . . before God the
Father hears my happiness! . . .

Now they are speaking once more:

Nina? What's the matter?

Nothing, dear. Nerves, that's all. I've gotten over-tired, I
guess.

Then you go right to bed, young lady! We'll excuse you.

All right, dear. I guess I do need to rest. Good night, you
bossy old thing, you!

Good night, darling.

Good night, Charlie.

That's a good girl! Good night, dear.

Good night, Ned.

Thank you. Good night.

Here they are: thought and utterance, utterance and thought,
brought vividly before us each in its own entity. You will note
that the audience is not required to divine the thought which
prompts the action. The thought is presented to us directly
before it becomes translated into action. The subjective experience of the characters is separated from their objective experience (for some reason the image comes to my mind of a house-

wife separating the yolk from the white of an egg) and the two elements are recombined in a new theatrical form.

O'Neill's brilliant scene points straight toward the drama that is to be. But now I add a final thought. Presently some new dramatist will see that subjective experience can be most clearly and truthfully expressed by means of the motion picture. And the characters of his drama will appear, simultaneously, on the stage and on the screen—living their outward and inward lives before us at the same time. This is the new drama I foresee.

For the sake of added clearness I will restate in the simplest possible terms what I have said so far. I believe that our contemporary drama still deals, for the most part, with objective experience. That this objective approach is the result of a photographic habit of mind, which, in turn, is closely linked with the development of the camera. That photographs have begun to move and speak, and that, in so doing, they have ceased to be an objective experience and have become a subjective experience. That our painters, and our novelists, and certain of our dramatists have begun to explore the subconscious element in ourselves and to express it directly in its own character before it becomes translated into action. That the motion picture is the ideal medium with which to interpret our subconscious experience; and that the drama of the future will deal not with objective experience or subjective experience but with both varieties of experience at the same time expressing our essential duality in a new theatrical idiom involving the simultaneous use of the stage and the screen.

The facts at our disposal seem to point to this conclusion with inescapable logic. What follows is pure speculation. I am speaking of a drama and a theatre which do not yet exist. Only a poet could do justice to such a prophecy. The new drama will display not only action but the thoughts which prompts the action—not only the deed but the emotion behind the deed. We shall see a continuous play and interplay between outward action and interior motive—the warp and woof of a new fabric. And for the first time in the history of the drama we shall see ourselves presented in our new wholeness which we are only just beginning to understand. The new drama, I might borrow a current expression and call it the "two-way" drama, will be presented on what I might call, in turn, a "two-way" stage. Objective experience will be interpreted by flesh-and-blood actors appearing on a stage which will resemble, more or less closely, the realistic stage we are familiar with today. But above, and behind, and around this stage a motion picture screen will be erected. And on it are thrown the shadow selves of the characters of the drama—living and moving as our thoughts and emotion live and move. Our attention is focused now on the stage, now on the screen, now on both stage and screen as the drama dwells upon outward or inward experience or upon outward and inward experience at the same time. How shall I tell you? How can I evoke this for you?

The images of the three weird sisters hover and scream above Macbeth and Banquo as they pause at the crossroads on the blasted heath:

> Flapping from out their condor wings
> Invisible woe![10]

then making themselves air into which they vanish. They manifest themselves out of the icy fear which hangs over the banquet scene—inducing, as it were, the apparition of Banquo on the stage below them.

The Tragedy of Richard III unrolls its hideous tapestry beneath a sky of madness—stabbed through with violent images of crowns that drip blood, and enormous heraldic white roses, and murdered princes, and kings, and queens wrapped in their winding sheets.

The spirit of Hamlet's father: "Unhouseled, disappointed, unaneled.", appears again and again throughout the play—a nervous excitation in Hamlet's mind. In the final scene the body of Hamlet is borne, like a soldier, to the platform. The stage darkens—is blotted out. The last peal of ordnance is shot off. Only a cold, clear, still sky remains—a winter night in Elsinore. A star falls.

Now a scene from a drama of our own time. We see a high, blank, stone wall. Against it stands a man—blindfolded, manacled. Across from him a firing squad. The order is given to present arms. The soldiers raise their rifles. There is a pause. The stage grows dim. On the screen above us a spot of vivid light writes a monstrous enlargement of the doomed mans cardiograph—the spasmodic, furious beating of his heart.

These foreshadowings are only the faintest and most halting intimations of what we may expect to see in the theatre when the new dramatist takes his material in hand and begins to make his great orchestrations of the seen and the unseen. I use this word, "orchestrations," deliberately. For as time goes on we are beginning to see that life is not a melody—a single lonesome tune—but a symphony of many themes played on many instruments. We hear a great deal today about the coming century of the common man. Presently, it is true, our outward life will be fuller and more abundant than anything we have ever dreamed. But the new century of the common man is actually the century of the common man's awakening into the mystery, and the terror, and the wonder of his own inner self. This is the way life is moving. We cannot hasten it, or hinder it, or alter it. It is a trend of the times—a part of the drift of history. Vistas of power open before us. We are turning inward, and in doing so we are finding out how much of us lives. We are finding out that we are not so small, or so petty, or so various, or so mean, as we seem to be. We know very little of the shadow side of ourselves as yet. But we know enough to know that the old gods dwell there, and the devils, and the daemons—the forces that shape our fate, our destiny, our horoscope. The new dramatist, like Prometheus: "will bring to light

these fiery shapes that were aforetime wrapped in darkness";
and on his stage he will give us a new conception of what life
means—man in relation to his own inner consciousness. For
it is not our outer life, alone, that has meaning for us today nor
our inner life, alone; but the living relationship between our
outer life and our inner life. And it is precisely *this living
relationship* that is the subject of the new drama.

In life, as we live it, our inner experience runs parallel to our
outer experience but seldom meets it. The two varieties of
experience are rarely fused. But the new drama will present to
us not only our life in relation to the world we live in but our
relation to our own inner dream. Here is its promise. Seeing
it; hearing it; experiencing it; we can become *whole* once more.

Lecture 2

The Art of the Theatre

It is pleasant to know that you have asked for me to talk to you about the thing I know best and love best—the theatre. I wish I could be sure that what I am going to say will benefit you in same way. I am speaking out of a theatre experience. Everything I am going to say should be thought of within that frame. I am speaking, for the most part, of things that are intangible; of things, more over, that are seldom discussed in the professional theatre. I shall speak of matters which directly concern you as they have concerned me. Perhaps you will be good enough to accept this talk as a ventilation of some ideas that have occurred to me in quiet, and silence, and that have been seasoned by much reflection.

I am talking to you about the theatre as an "Art." I never talk about it in any other way. I never think about it in any other way. And I am talking to you about the American theatre. The American theatre is my business, and it is your business. The European theatre can get along very well without our help. We may remember with profit to ourselves, if not exactly with pride, that the most significant production of recent seasons—*Oedipus Rex*[1]—was written by a Greek, adapted by an Irishman, directed by a Frenchman, and acted by Englishmen; and that America had nothing to do with it except to furnish a rather inadequate playhouse for it. It is the American theatre that we are interested in. But I must say, frankly, that however deeply we may believe in the future of the art of the theatre in this country; the art of the theatre in this country, at this time, is very hard to find. We all have our memories, in my case enchanted memories, of a theatre that is gone. We all have our hopes and our dreams of a theatre which is to be. But when we attempt to discuss the theatre of the present day with any seriousness we discover at once that we have very little to discuss. What we are practicing today in the name of theatre has almost nothing to do with the theatre. It is so unrelated to real theatre that sometimes it actually seems as if you would have to grow a new set of faculties to create theatre with. This thing that I am saying is not a whim, nor a beef, nor a gripe. It is a fact. What we are taught to call theatre today isn't theatre at all. True theatre isn't, with the rarest exceptions, to be found in our playhouses. It has gone out of the window. It has hidden itself bitterly away.

I realize that this statement is a challenging one. I think we have no choice but to accept it. All we have to do is to look at what is going on in our theatre. There is no doubt that we have come to be satisfied with a very inferior grade of goods. Life at this moment is unbelievably dramatic. Glance through the columns of any newspaper. Listen to any broadcast. Read the morning's mail. Pick up the telephone. Drama is all around us—in the very air we breathe. But the odd thing is, it isn't in the theatre. In the face of the almost unbearable tensions of our everyday living, the thing that is happening behind the proscenium arches of our playhouses inevitably seems harmless, and tepid, and cute beyond words. A "patty-cake theatre", I sometimes call it. There is something in our theatre like a miasma, like a conspiracy, that seems to make us shy away from profound and passionate emotions. We miss the qualities that give "a noble turn to things." We miss the freshness, the caprice, the splendor, the austerity, the elevation; what H.L. Mencken calls, "the grand crash and glitter . . . "; what Isak Dinesen calls, "the gleam, grandezza, the wild hope." But these extravagant qualities are the life blood of the theatre—the sap, the vital fluid. Without them the theatre ebbs away into Broadway show-business. There is something in our theatre that is synthetic, ersatz, second-hand—copying copies of copies, reflecting reflected reflections. It has a kind of hearsay quality. Our contemporary theatre tells us, with great clearness and expertness, what theatre would be like if it were only "theatre." It reminds us of the crack made by Margaret Halsey, in the days when jeering at England was still fashionable, that English women's shoes looked as if they had been made by somebody who had heard of a shoe but had never seen one. I am not talking about show-business, remember; I am talking about the theatre as an "art." I am talking about creation, a terrifying word—creation—the little shy flickering flame of life. I am talking about ardor, and wonder, and innocence, and horror, and despair, and things that are haunted and fraught with dreams, and magnificences, and raptures, and glories. I am talking about the beating of the human heart in the theatre and the pulsing of life along its veins. And I am saying that the life of the theatre is almost extinguished. The flame is burning alarmingly low. I think it is for young people everywhere to cherish and nurture that flame and try to bring back life into the theatre. I think you have to try. We must have great emotions in the theatre. Otherwise it isn't theatre. I didn't make that law. It is an old, old law. It *is* so!

The business of workers in the theatre is, as I see it, to express a timeless theme by means of the tools of one's own time. And we are not using the tools of our own time in the theatre. I do not mean that we are neglecting the motion

picture, or the radio, or television. That is not what I mean at
all. I mean that we are not using the idiom of our own time.
And by "idiom" I do not mean the actual language of our time.
I mean that the manner of our thinking and feeling in the
theatre is neither so good nor so alive as our way of thinking
and feeling outside the theatre. All we have to do is to look
about us at what is being done in other artistic fields, and then
to look at what is being done in the theatre, to realize at once
that the idiom of the theatre is strikingly out of date. Our way
of expressing ourselves in the theatre is years behind the
times—years and years. I must confess that I do not know the
reason for this time lag. But lately I have observed a curious
fact. We have all had it dinned into our ears that the theatre
is always being "reborn" and that it can "never die." I think
we can take it for granted, by now, that the theatre is here to
stay. It follows, then, that the changing conventions of the
theatre—Expressionism, for example, Constructivism, The
Living Newspaper, Existentialism, and so on—are in the nature of fashions that come and go, like the Merry Widow Hat,
or the straight-front corset, or the Zoot Suit. Just now it is the
fashion to say that our theatre is in a state of flux, that it has
no form at all. But, as a matter of fact, I think the opposite is
true. Our theatre seems to me to have a very definite form, a
very definite set of conventions. And these conventions are so
widespread and so all-inclusive that it is sometimes even dif-
ficult to distinguish one play from another, or even to know
which theatre we are in. The plays are so alike in plot and in
treatment. The setting is so standardized. The actors all look
so alike, and stand, and sit, and walk, and talk in so much the
same way. And the set, the sets, look so alike. It is these conventions that are outdated. They would serve just as well for a
production of *Uncle Tom's Cabin* as for a production of *Deep
Are The Roots.* [2] We have no medium at hand with which to
express a contemporary situation in theatre terms, no contemporary medium, that is. This is true, I think, and it is sad. For

it means that the theatre has forgotten its audience. It has taken liberties with its audience.

Meanwhile the world is moving. Speaking out about my own experience, I cannot help feeling that it is partly our persistent clinging to the realistic approach to the theatre that has kept us all so backward. All my life I have been opposed to realism in the theatre, but I have never been able to put my objections into words with complete satisfaction even to myself. Not long ago I came across this sentence. I quote it with pleasure, for it seems to say precisely what I would like to say:

What is called realism is usually a record of life at a low pitch and ebb viewed in the sunless light of day.

This is exactly my feeling. There is nothing wrong with realism in the theatre, not a thing. The arguments in favor of it are far too many and far too powerful for me to try to demolish. Nothing that I could possibly say would influence it in the slightest. But I cannot escape the conviction, which has grown stronger and more insistent through the years, that realism in the theatre is an infallible sign of low vitality. Just as elaborate scenic productions are an infallible sign of low vitality in the theatre. Realism is something we practice when we aren't feeling very well. When we don't feel up to making the extra effort. So we just come home, and sit down by the fire, and put on our slippers, and pat the dog, and stroke the cat, and open our copy of Bartlett's *Familiar Quotations* and our album of candid camera shots. And then if we are playwrights we write plays filled with ice boxes, and toast-racks, and laundries. And if we are actors we slouch on and off the stage, and loll on sofas, and tap cigarettes. And if we are stage designers we just design another of those tasteful, well-furnished rooms with one wall missing. It is all so easy, so lazy, so timid. But when we are full of energy, when we feel in trim and in tune, we go up on the mountain top where the great wind blows and give ourselves up to the keen, heady joy that only the exercise of the imagination can give us and watch it blaze and flame. Then we are in the high rare atmosphere of great theatre art, and we write:

> If I quench thee, thou flaming minister
> I can again thy former light restore,
> Should I repent me . . .[3]

And we say:

> I am dying, Egypt, dying; only
> I here importune death awhile, until
> Of many thousand kisses the poor last
> I lay upon thy lips.[4]

And we feel the elation that Duse felt when she wrote on the margin of the last act of *Rosmersholm*, "The moon, the moon, the moon! Folly! Madness! Love! Death!." Flames into thought.

I understand very well that the controversy over the function of realism in our theatre will not be brought to an end by any opinions I may express. But, again speaking personally, I must confess that I have found this linking of realism with weakness and timorousness and general lack of vitality most heartening in times of doubt. Art, we many remember, is an imitation of the nature of things not of their appearances. Perhaps it would be truer to speak of realism in the theatre as a symptom of backwardness rather than as a cause of backwardness.

Another symptom of backwardness, it seems to me, is our antiquated and childish idea of exposition in the theatre. It has got so that the first twenty minutes of any topical play are a guessing contest between the playwright and his audience. Somebody on the stage says, "Oh, hello, Mazie!" and immediately we tumble to the fact that her name is "Mazie". Then, gradually, we are treated to a list of the necessary data of the play. We are allowed to "horn in" on them, so to speak. Presently, when we are all worn out with this embarrassing display of the "tag-you're-it" technique, the real drama begins. It is all so tiresome, so feeble, so creaky. Let's do away with the hocus-pocus and get back to the theatre's age old, ageless, business of creating life. It is so easy, if you would just have a little courage. For example: why don't you have the leading character of your next play stand alone on a bare stage at the rise of the curtain and say right out, "I'm Joe Dokes, age 34, married, with a couple of kids," etc.; and then roll up his sleeves, and tread the boards, and begin to act. Or, to carry this line of thought even further, why not a play composed entirely of soliloquies, allowing an audience to build up the plot in its own mind? And so on.

Perhaps the most striking symptom of the theatre's failure to keep abreast of the times is the way we mistake efficiency—expertness—for true creation. Americans are "gadget-minded." We have the "know-how," as we say. And it is precisely because we have the know how, because we are so keenly interested in expertness and efficiency; that we are apt to confuse these qualities with true creation. There is no doubt that our American theatre is the most expert theatre in the world—the snappiest, the slickest. So expert, in fact, that a distinguished European visitor spoke of it not long ago as a "clinical theatre." We write our plays, we act our roles, we design and build our productions as if they were so many triumphs of mechanical skill—like the Big Inch, or the George Washington Bridge, or the Grand Coulee Dam. The Broadway of today is like an exhibit of engines. But the theatre isn't an engine. It's an organism. It's alive. It lives and breathes. And its wild, wild, strange, uncontrollable! It won't allow itself to be reduced to mechanical terms. In the face of our efficiency writing, efficiency acting, efficiency staging, and setting, and lighting; the theatre just simply isn't there. Something else is there—something entertaining, doubtless; and charming, and amusing, and interesting, and all that. But where is the authentic theatre thrill? And where is the "awe"? And where is the "glory"? Did you ever hear anyone use the word "glory" before in connection with the theatre? But you should hear it. You should experience glory in the theatre. It is your right as a member of an audience.

One thing that is wrong, so far as you and I are concerned, is that we think of the various branches of the theatre as separate entities. We think of a play as a manuscript and not as theatre. Yes, we do! We think of a stage setting as a set and not as theatre. We think of lighting in terms of a remarkable electric console and not in terms of theatre. We cannot seem to grasp the conception that all these departments, perhaps I should have said compartments, of the theatre are organic parts of an organic whole, not a set of commissions efficiently carried out; but a nervous, temperamental, vibrating, living whole. I have just used the word "nervous." I like to us the word "nervous" in connection with the theatre. I don't mean nervous in a neurotic sense. I am speaking of an energy of the nerves—the sheer nervous vitality that runs like a fever through Michelangelo's frescoes in the Sistine Chapel; that makes Hamlet say:

> Here, thou incestuous, murderous, damned Dane,
> Drink off this potion.

The "nerveux," Henry Adams calls it.

Much of the difficulty comes, it seems to me, from our being so job-conscious in America. Each separate part of the theatre is just a separate job to be done. Take stage designing, for instance. When I began work in the theatre I assumed, as a matter of course, that a stage designer was supposed to take entire charge of the visual side of the theatre. Even now, I would not dream of committing anyone else to design the costumes or arrange the lighting for any play I happen to be working on. But I am told that nowadays stage designers don't care who designs the costumes or arranges the lighting of their shows. I must confess that I don't understand this at all. It seems to me to be a part of our present day tendency to disintegrate, to dissolve: Scenery by Blank, Shoes by Dash, Lighting by Black, Costumes by Whosis, Coiffures by Charles of the Ritz, Makeup by Max Factor, Fingernails by Madame So-and-So, Ashtrays by Orientalia, Entrances by Je Ne Sais Quoi, Exits by Was Geschieht, Smiles by Whatever, Frowns by Wherever, and so on, and so on. I wonder where it will end? But to tell the truth, I am not greatly interested in the theatre that is endable. Nor am I greatly interested in critical appraisals of one kind of theatre or another kind of theatre. We tend to accept our present theatrical forms as inevitable. But they aren't inevitable at all. On the contrary. The clever, sapless, juiceless, greedy theatre we are accustomed to will disappear in time, unremembered for the most part, and another theatre with a larger and healthier idea will take its place. I think it is clear that unless we are willing to continue in the same, old, sterile routine; stuck fast in yesterday like poor Jim Jay in the nursery rhyme: "Ho diddle di do, poor Jim Jay, Got stuck fast in yesterday," we shall have to break down our mental adhesions and move boldly into a new theatrical experience. We shall have to evolve a new way of looking at the theatre. We shall have to learn, not how things are being done in the theatre, but how they might be done. Not only how they might be done, but how they might best be done. We shall have to stop acquiring information and begin, instead, to acquire an attitude. I'm going to say that again: Not information, but an attitude! Not a catalog, but a new point of view. We shall have to get a truer mental image of the theatre and what it is for.

Well, you may ask, what is the theatre for? I can only speak of the theatre as I see it. To me the theatre is a source of energy—a well-spring of *energy*. To use the modern scientific terms we all love to use, we go to the theatre to get "re-charged," exactly as a storage battery is re-charged, by the electric current of emotion that streams from the stage. The illustration is an apt one. Why, otherwise, should actors be so exhausted at the end of a performance? Surely not from a mere recitation of the playwright's words. All our effort as workers in the theatre must be to learn to throw the energy, the sense of life, out across the footlights—more excitement, more beauty, more splendor, more and more energy, more and more life, more aliveness! Someone once wrote a review of a play in which he spoke of the production as "a humming mountain of fire!" I've remembered that phrase for years. But it takes *life* to create life in the theatre. That is our difficulty We don't seem to be able to experience anything. We only learn *about* it. We close ourselves to experience. We shut ourselves away from it. We insulate ourselves against it. We don't look! We don't listen! Why can't we learn to use our eyes and our ears? Why can't we at least learn to be aware of what is going on around us?

I feel an impulse to speak further about this matter. It is quite possible for us to lead a completely fulfilled life in this country, at this moment; if we only have a job, and a home with a bathroom, and a radio, and a car, and can go to the movies every Saturday night, and play a game of pinochle every so often with the boys. Oh yes, I forgot the comics; we must have the comics. Thousands of Americans, tens of thousands of Americans, are living happily and contentedly with no inner life at all. Why bother? It will do no harm for us to remember, at this point, that Shakespeare didn't have a car, or a radio; and neither did Sophocles; and neither did Moliere.

I will tell you of an experience I had in the theatre at Epidaurus, in Greece, some years ago. You can read about Epidaurus in Henry Miller's remarkable book, *The Colossus of Maroussi*. The Colossus of Maroussi, by the way is not a statue; but a man—the modern Greek poet, Katsimbalis. Everything you've heard about this theatre is true. Its proportions are flawless. Its acoustics are miraculous. Its surroundings are beautiful beyond words—with a strange Greek beauty of bare hills and light. They've told you all this. What they have not told you is that just around the corner, just out of range of the camera, lie the ruins of the ancient Temple of Hippocrates with its healing mineral springs, and its museum of surgical instruments, and its rare manuscripts. Here was the medical center of the civilized world—the Johns Hopkins of Ancient Greece, its Mayo Clinic. And it is obvious, as obvious as a pump handle or a sore thumb; obvious, that is to anyone except the pedants, that this great theatre was not only a theatre but a lecture hall and an operating clinic as well. Just as simple as that. I saw all this, and then, in a sudden flash of perception, I saw how the drama was used in this place as an active agent of healing. I felt the subtle elixirs in the air around me. I saw the rows of patients gathered in the theatre to witness a fare-well performance of one of the great Greek dramas before being sent back to take their places again in the world—ex-posed in one last climax of emotion to the curative, and inspir-iting, and strengthening consciousness of their gods and their country. And I felt for the first time the dramatic impact of *Prometheus*, and *Ion*, and *Oedipus*, and the rest, considered not as performances but as ceremonies. Sitting there in that sacred place it all seemed natural to me—the normal way of things. I saw the immense power of these old dramas. That day Greek drama took on a new meaning for me. Imagine a public art undivorced, as yet, from religion and from polity. How un-meaning and how personal the theatre has become when we regard *Oedipus* today merely as the harrowing story of a hand-some young man in a dreadful predicament.

It is impossible, of course, to give you a set of rules by which we may create a theatre that exists as yet only in dreams. But as we work towards this theatre there are certain truths which we shall do well to keep in mind. Here is one of them. *Art is not like life, only better; art is different from life. And artists are different from laymen.* There is a creative state of mind; and there is a creative state of feeling. There is a peculiar point of view, a special point of view, a special way of looking at things that creative people know and share with one another. And the creative way of looking at things isn't like the ordinary way of looking at things, only clearer. It's different. It's "other." The great artists of the world don't see things the way we do. They don't, as the expression goes, "see eye-to-eye" with us. Aeschylus, Ben Jonson, Eleanora Duse, yes; and Michelangelo, and Bach, and Dante had perceptions that we don't have. Their way of looking at things is not our way. So an important step toward real creation in the theatre is to implant this truth in our minds. Art isn't just better; it's different. Another thing to keep in mind is: that *the theatre deals with emotion and not with reason. It is a thing of the heart and not a thing of the head*. I urge you to remember this, and put it down in your notebooks, and think of it often. I will give you an example. The play, *Othello*, as you all know, is the story of an over-mastering emotion—the emotion of jealousy—growing and growing until it brings the characters down at the close of the play in one general ruin. Now from the point of view of reason and logic, Othello is just a sap. If he had had an iota of sense he would have taken Desdemona and Iago and Emila with him to a psychoanalyst (in this case to their father-confessor as Romeo and Juliet went to Friar Lawrence) and they would have aired their various tendencies and trends and inhibitions, and their troubles would have been over at once. But then there would have been no play. So much for logic in the theatre.

Another thing to keep in mind is the difference between imagination and ingenuity in the theatre. The difference is a subtle one but a profound one. *Imagination is the God-given faculty of "thinking up things." Ingenuity is the sworn enemy of imagination—in the theatre or out of it. Ingenuity not only destroys imagination, it destroys our capacity for imagination.* It was imagination that wrote *Green Pastures*. It was ingenuity that cooked up *Lady In The Dark*. Do you see the difference? Still another thing for us to remember is the difference between public art and private art. *The art of the theatre is a public art*. At the risk of quoting what must be pretty much of an "old wheeze" by now, let me remind you that someone once said: "Speech has two purposes: relief and communication." Now, trite as that remark is, we still don't seem to understand it very well in the theatre. Many of our modern plays are not communicated to their audiences. They are not given to the public. They remain private. They are the playwright's business, and the actor's business; but they obstinately remain not our business. They are like surreptitious chuckles, or jokes told by deaf mutes, or, when they are serious, they are like cries of distress far away and half heard. But the theatre belongs to the crowd— *la foule*. What a pity that the excitement that should be in the theatre should be found only in baseball parks, and arenas, and stadiums, and race courses—the crowd, *la foule*, the savage monster.

And now I am going to speak of strange and secret matters for a moment. Matters, which like the secrets in Edgar Allen Poe's *Ligeia*, are "too divinely precious not to be forbidden." We write our plays, and send them to an agent; and presently they are accepted and produced; and we come to the opening night; and the aisles are lined with critics; and turntables go round and round; and lights go on and off; and curtains go up and down; and morning papers carry rave reviews that are blown-up in ten thousand dollar ads in later editions. But the crowd—the beast—the wonderful, terrible, satanic, angelic animal still sleeps—untroubled, undisturbed, unawakened! What new dramatist will presently appear to awake, and arouse, and dominate this creature? Why are the demagogues and the dictators the only people today with a real sense of theatre? Why are we incapable of seeing that the dramatist can do all that they can? That he can arouse fervor, and frenzy, and sacrifice, and unquestioning belief in multitudes as they did—and all for good. I am speaking of mysteries now—dark things, marvelous things, inestimable stones, unvalued jewels. And I will not say any more, except to remind you that in the face of this heart-shaking vision of what the theatre might become—a shining thing, a light to the world—our little safe, tepid, competent theatre seems mild indeed. But I think we should not take our little, safe, tepid, competent theatre for granted. There are better dreams.

And now I will give you the very greatest example of theatre that I know. The Italian poet-dramatist, Gabriele D'Annunzio, once wrote a novel, *Il Fuoco*, *The Flame Of Life*, in which he makes the great actress, la Foscarina, tell how she played Juliet in the old Roman amphitheater in Verona. Here is her story:

> I had bought a . . . bunch of roses with my little savings in the Piazza delle Erbe, under the fountain of Madonna Verona. The roses were my only ornament. I mingled them with my words, with my gestures, with each attitude of mine. I let one fall at the feet of Romeo when we first met; I strewed the leaves of another on his head from the balcony; and I covered his body with the whole of them in the tomb.

Now, Foscarina was Eleanora Duse. How many thousands of actresses have played the role of Juliet since the play was written? Who but Duse ever saw so deep into its meaning? And yet, how simple this is. Anyone might have thought of it. No modernistic scenery, no interlocking dimmer boxes, no devices of the new stagecraft; only a girl carrying an armful of white roses and the life-giving dramatic imagination. Juliet: a flower, a rose, a white rose; blooming, fading, scattered:

Sweet flower, with flowers thy bridal bed I strew—[5]

By this one gesture, a gesture of excelling simplicity, the actress unified and exalted the human tragedy of boy and girl passion into a great natural happening. She made it a part of nature—like a flower, like the earth, like the evening. Her truth shone on the play like a beam of light.

She continues her story. The day, she says:

> was a quiet one, like today. . . . The sky was very far, yet now and then it seemed as if my weakest words must sound in its farthest distances, . . . The crowd . . . sat silent on the curved steps that were now in shadow. Above it the top of the wall was still red. I was telling of the terror of day, but I already felt 'the mask of night' on my face. . . . The tragedy was hurrying on. I still have the memory of a great sky white as pearls, and of a noise as of the sea that quieted down when I appeared; and of the smell of pitch that came from the torches . . . And of a distant sound of bells that brought the sky nearer to us, and of that sky that was losing its light little by little as I was losing my life, and of a star, the first star, that trembled in my eyes with my tears.

Moments like these are what we must look at if we are to learn about the theatre, for the life of the theatre is in them.

Suppose you were to ask me, each one of you, with that reasonableness which seems to me to be the most admirable and most endearing of qualities, the typical American question: "Well, what do you want me to do?" Suppose for once I try to answer that question? Suppose I said to myself: "After all, I am among friends. We are all interested in the same thing. What do I want? What do I really want you to do?" I will tell you. I want you *not* to believe the thing you have grown up to believe. The thing you have been taught to believe. That the theatre is a petty, clever, slick, cheap place. I want you to put an end to this sterile idea. I want you to realize that the life of the theatre can be larger and more vital than anything you have ever known. I want you to realize that you have been misled by watching the starved, warped output of the Broadway theatre, until you have taken it for granted that the theatre is something less than the terrible, wonderful, flaming thing it is. I want you to know that your life in the theatre can be full, can be rich, can be drunken with beauty and power; and that elation can be your daily life, your daily bread. I want you to get a sense of responsibility towards the theatre. I want you to realize that what you *are* shows through what you *do* in the theatre. I want you to move out of the shallows into the deep current. I want you to acknowledge the fundamental mystery of the theatre. I want you to learn that observation is not a substitute for insight; that ingenuity is not a substitute for imagination; that cleverness is not a substitute for culture. I want you to realize that we are beginning to see that America and Americans are not in the least like what we thought they were. And I want you to create in the theatre out of this new awareness of ourselves and of our country. I want you to realize how deficient we are in a sense of reality, and how we try to compensate for this deficiency in all sorts of dazzling and futile ways. I want you to learn how the reactions of an audience differ from the reactions of every individual in that audience. I want to repeat that. I want you to learn how the reactions of an audience differ from the reactions of every individual in that audience. I want you to know that audiences have capacities for feeling that no dramatist has ever touched. I want you to learn the heightened perception—the contagious excitement—out of which all great work for the theatre is created. I want you to learn to see life dynamically—to see it in motion, to see it in action. I want you to learn to respond to the livingness that is in each fleeting instant of time. To become aware, and always more aware, of that livingness until at last you can know what Plato calls, "the madness of those possessed by the Muses." More than anything else, I want you to be true to your dreams of the theatre. Now, at your time of life, is when you acquire them. Never go back on them. Never! Be true to your dreams. Be true to your love. Be true to your love.

We get the impression from what we see in our theatres and what we read in our newspapers that the theatre is hardly worth bothering about. That it has long since ceased to be an exercise for adult minds. The opinion of theatre is a discouraged one. We look in vain for aspiration, even for encouragement. The feeling is jaded and sorrowful. Why have we imagined ourselves into anything so poor, and mean, and low? You are young. You are strong. You are daring. Make your choice now. Don't be satisfied with what you see in the theatre. Don't accept the counsels of a theatre that is dominated by the spirit of compromise. Don't accept what is offered you by frustrated, disillusioned, unhappy people. Don't let this be! Abandon a theatre whose natural condition is fear. And move into a theatre whose natural condition is ecstasy! Realize that the theatre is incessantly changing, incessantly moving into something new, and fresh, and young—a theatre where it is always morning. And know that here is your only peace, your only joy, your only rest.

I am here to remind you of this tremendous affirmation. Let your theatre be heart-broken. Let it be tragic. Let it be filled with groping and blackness. But don't let it be feeble. Don't let it be obtuse. Don't let it be unaware. Enlarge your ideas, your emotions, your conceptions. Let your imaginations be dilated. Let the dynamis of the true artist enter into you. Take the little gift you have into the hall of the gods. Have you never seen the intent expression on the faces of audiences at the theatre when they are at one with the performance, when they are safe in the vital current of the performance, off their guard, all defenses laid aside, wrapped in the moment, their souls in their eyes?

I think of a tale by Olaf Stapledon, *Last and First Men*. It begins in the manner of the science fiction romances one reads in *Astounding Stories*, but then it grows and grows and it ends in speculations almost too vast to comprehend. Mr. Stapledon traces the progress of mankind through eons of triumph and despair. At last, untold billions of years hence, when the universe is darkening down to its final end; a great teacher sums up the meaning of human life. "It was like a melody," he says.

That is our story. We are here for a little while between mystery and mystery. We live for a little time on this earth that is so fair. Could we, here, theatre-minded, protean as we are; could we sense for a brief moment the melody of our being? And having sensed it could we impart it to our fellow men? Follow this dream into the light. The road is long but the rewards at the end are greater than you know. Take with you as you go the words of Plato:

> For those who have once set foot upon the upward pilgrimage do not go down again to darkness and to journey beneath the earth, but they live in light, always.

Lecture 3

Why We Have Theatres

I would like to tell you about something that happened to me one afternoon last summer during the baseball season. I was walking up Fifth. Avenue and I heard an odd, snarling noise ahead of me. It was a man walking alone with a walkie-talkie on his shoulder. He was following the ball game at the Yankee Stadium and the growls and screams were his excited comments, "Trow Da Bum Out!" I said to myself, "This is really contemporary. This man isn't going to be satisfied any longer with the work of Maxwell Anderson or Arthur Miller, or even of Tennessee Williams. I wonder what would satisfy him in the theatre?" Certainly something new.

Now let me tell you about something that happened to me at one of our great western universities. When my lecture was finished a young man came up to me, very angry:

"I paid a dollar to hear you just now." he said.

"Well," I said, "I'm sunk right there, because I don't think anybody's opinion about anything is worth a dollar these days. Besides, I thought this talk was free."

"No, it wasn't free." he said, "We each paid a dollar to hear you. And for that dollar I thought I was going to find out how to get a job. And all I got was a lecture." Then he went away.

I have thought of this little episode many times—many, many times, and always with sadness. The kind of theatre this young man had in mind—how did he get this idea? Who gave it to him? The great flourishing institution filled with limitless opportunities for a bright young man—that kind of theatre died years ago. It just up and died. There isn't any such theatre anymore.

If I had to choose one word, and only one, with which to characterize our American theatre I would say that that word would be the word "cute." What a strange word to use about anything American. What a strange word to use about the theatre. Time and time again of late I've asked myself the question: How is it possible that we, in this great country, can be willing to accept such a second-rate notion of the theatre? Where shall we find the elation, the ferment, the vibration, the restless searching, the eager questioning, the insatiable curiosity, the incessant reaching out for new and vital forms of theatrical expression that should be inseparably bound up with this, the greatest of all the arts?

We do not need to listen to the Delphic Oracle, or to a reading of the tea leaves in a Gypsy tea room to learn that the professional theatre at this time is not in the best of health. But as we watch its death struggles—at least they appear to be its death struggles—we see that more and more people are beginning to dream about a new theatre in this country, and to concern themselves with their own relation to it. I observe that audiences—audiences interested in the theatre, that is—are very serious these days. I feel that this is as it should be. For in the past twenty-five years—more than two whole generations, that is—there has not been one single new creative impulse in any branch of the American theatre—not one. So with your permission we will get down to business. I will try hard to be clear.

A list of books—"unrequired" reading—might be helpful to you at this point. Here are some of the books I read over and over again. They are not orthodox. First of all there is Emma Sheridan Frye's *Educational Dramatics,* one of the best books on the theatre I know. Here is one sentence from it: "A director must direct." There is more in this than meets the eye. There is D. H. Lawrence's *Studies In Classic American Literature.* Laugh this statement off if you can: "The essential American soul is hard, isolate, stoic, and a killer. It has never been melted." There are Gertrude Stein's books, *Narration* and *Lectures In America*, with their remarkable discussions of the time element in the theatre. There is Dr. Carl Jung's series of lectures given at Yale University in 1937, the "Terry Lectures," published under the title, *Psychology And Religion*. There is the latest book on Melville, *Call Me Ishmael*, with its astonishing proposition that the Pacific Ocean is an American lake. Do you realize, by the way, that it was America who opened Japan to world trade, with guns, a hundred years ago. And that it was America who bombed Hiroshima a hundred years later after Japan had been opened. There is a drama for you. It's terrific! It's dynamite! It's atomic! Try and get it written. Try and get it produced. Read Amy Lowell's *Guns As Keys* and *The Great Gate Swings*. There is Professor Kernodle's fascinating book, *From Art To Theatre.* There is *Behold, This Dreamer!* by Walter De le Mare, a book that is like a great river of thought. And there is a little known and still untranslated book by Adolphe Appia, *The Living Art*, a study, *the* study, in fact, of light in the theatre. Which makes us realize again that stage lighting is a matter of musical temperament and not a matter of mechanism. Here is my little list; and a good one it is. On second thought, I will add to this list, *Plays And Controversies*, by William Butler Yeats. I consider that the Abbey Theatre Company was the most important theatrical company of its time, not excepting the famous company of the Moscow Art Theatre. Here are the stimulating records of this theatre's beginnings. I have read and re-read this book many, many times. The extraordinary thing is that the Abbey Theatre came into being as a "poet's theatre." And that it is as a "poet's theatre" that it has become known all over the world.

Now, the first thing I want to talk about is "excitement." You all know who Gertrude Stein was, and whether or not you agree with the way in which she expressed her opinions, I think you cannot help agreeing with her statement that the business of an artist is to be exciting. I'm going to say that again: "The business of an artist is to be exciting." That sentence ought to be heard everyday, on every radio station, every hour on the hour, like a singing commercial: "THE BUSINESS OF AN ARTIST IS TO BE EXCITING!"

I will tell you a story about excitement. I came across this story in a history of the gold rush days in California, a hundred years ago. The theatre of that time, as you know, had an unusual social vitality. One of its ornaments was a lanky boy of 19 named Edwin Booth, who had come up across Texas and got himself a job playing character parts in a famous repertory company in Sacramento. My story concerns a performance of Shakespeare's *Coriolanus* given by that company. According to the chronicle, the performance was a very exciting one indeed. The reason it was so exciting was that the front row of the balcony was filled with miners, who sat with their guns trained on the stage over the balcony rail, repeating the lines of the play aloud, by heart, as the play went on; and shooting at the feet of the actors whenever they missed a word or a cue. That is one way to get excitement in the theatre. But it is not the only way; nor is it the only kind of excitement. The kind of excitement I am talking about is an excitement that comes from within. It is self-generated. It needs no stimulus from outside. This excitement, the theatre excitement—the unmistakable theatre thrill—occurs only in the presence of profound and passionate emotions. The qualities that give a noble turn to things. Without them the theatre withers away into show business. But I am not talking about show business. I am talking about ardor, and wonder, and horror, and despair, and things that are haunted and fraught with dreams, and magnificences, and raptures, and glories. I am talking about the beating of the human heart in the theatre and the pulsing of life along the veins. We must have great emotions in the theatre.

You are talented enough. That isn't what the trouble is. I am not speaking to stupid people. Our trouble is older and deeper—far older, far deeper. Without knowing it we have allowed ourselves to become a part of the debasing, cheapening process of American life. What a shameful thing to have to say. And now we are thinking of the theatre in terms of a job to be done—a first-night success, a sheaf of rave reviews—and never in terms of an experience to be imparted. Our theatre is a prose theatre—reportorial, journalistic. And the natural result—a natural, simple, inevitable reaction—is that the theatre has ceased to hold the attention of the public. For the theatre is either great or it is nothing. We must not make the mistake of blaming the movies, or the radio, or television for the decline of the theatre. We must blame the theatre for the decline of the theatre. It has not been destroyed by hostile outside influences. It has rotted away from within.

As I said in the beginning, we are here to try to establish some basic and workable truths with regard to a new theatre. The theatre to many of us is a building. But the new theatre I'm talking about is not a building, but a dream—a new concept, a new point of view. We are apt these days to confuse construction with creation. This confusion is well worth thinking about. It is at the heart of our contemporary American dilemma. Let's get this straight in our minds. To construct is one thing, but to create is quite another thing.

We are here, I repeat, to try to establish, if we can, some

basic and workable truths with regard to a new theatre. Let us
begin by asking ourselves the simplest of questions: *What is the
theatre and what is it for?* Do you know, [that] no two people
agree as to the answer to this question, [that] there are as many
differing opinions as to the nature and the purpose and the
function of the theatre as there are people in this audience? For
example: Is our new theatre to be the aesthetic theatre of Gor-
don Craig, the orgiastic theatre of Max Reinhardt, the static
theatre of Gertrude Stein, the propaganda theatre of the Rus-
sians, the clinical theatre of Arthur Miller and Tennessee Williams, or the musical theatre of Rodgers and Hammerstein? Is
it opera? Is it ballet? Is it the motion picture? Is it radio? Is it
television? Will it be the theatre of Arthur Hopkins, the theatre
of Moss Hart, the theatre of Thornton Wilder, the theatre of
Ruth Draper, the theatre of Agna Enters, the theatre of Martha
Graham? Is it all of these, or any of them, or none of them?
What is the basis? What is the lowest common denominator?
The fact is that today no two people have the same mental
image of the theatre. Now this is very serious, and it always
amazes and disturbs me. For how can we create in the theatre
without a common conception of the theatre to inspire us? The
answer is: We can't; we don't; we only make time. But I think
that if we were to hold a general discussion and sort our
conclusions, and sift them, and re-sift them, we might come in
the end to something like this; "All arts deal with life!" Of
course they do. In fact, this is what we call, where I come from,
an "old wheeze": "*All arts deal with life!*"[1] Any art that did not
deal with life would be a dead art. But the art of the theatre is
the art which deals directly with life. Its material is the stuff of
life itself. If music can be called the art of the sound of life, if
painting can be called the art of the look of life, if literature can
be called the art of the recording of life, then the art of the
theatre can be called the art of the *living* of life. Life itself,
transformed into art, in our presence, before our eyes. In using
these high sounding words I am running the risk of seeming

to be lost in a cloud of vague mysticism. But actually I am talking about something exact and definite.

I am going to make myself clear by using a very simple illustration—so simple it is almost grotesque. I have here an ordinary white china cup—bought at the department store for a few cents. Now there are many different ways in which we may look at this cup. For example, let us suppose that you are a very young child. You'll have a few elementary, naive reactions as you look at it. You will say, "Cup." You will say, "My cup." You will say, "White, round, drink, milk, mine," and that is all. Now let us suppose that you are a painter: a man like Grant Wood, let us say, or Matisse, or Stuart Davis. You will look at the cup with a painter's eye. You will be interested primarily in its appearance. You will see it, not as something to drink from, but as a pattern—a kind of map of light and dark areas of color. You will try to arrange these areas on your canvas so as to create a set of visual harmonies which you will call a picture. Placing this curve against that curve, this light against this shadow, this mass of white in relation to the rectangular frame that encloses it; and so on—an arrangement of colored shapes: a picture. Now let us suppose that you are a scientist looking at this cup. You will see it in still another way. You will begin to investigate at once with a scientist's curiosity. You will begin to ask questions. What is this cup made of? What is it made for? Why is it round? How much does it weigh? How much does it hold? How do we drink? And so on. You will be interested in the function of the cup, its properties, its uses, the manner in which it is designed to fulfill its purposes. This may lead you into discussions of pottery making—of moulding and firing and glazing, of the psychological satisfactions of drinking, and so on. But now, in this series of pretendings, let us suppose that you are that odd creature, a man of the theatre. You will see the cup "in action." You will not snatch at it, as a child might do, You will not regard it as a subject of a painting or a story or a poem, as a painter might do. You will not inquire into its nature or its uses, as a scientist might do. You will see it in the act of being used. The immediate importance of the cup is the thing that will interest you—its importance at this particular moment. Images will rush up in your mind when you look at it—images of scenes in which a cup has played a part. Here is one of them:

Now the hour of sunset was near . . . Soon the jailer . . . entered and stood by him saying:—To you, Socrates, whom I know to be the noblest and gentlest and best who ever came to this place, I will not impute the angry feelings of other men, who rage and swear at me when in obedience to the authorities I bid them drink the poison . . . for others, as you are aware, and not I, are the guilty cause. And so fare you well and try to bear lightly what must needs be—you know my errand.

Then bursting into tears, he turned away and went out.

Socrates looked after him and said: I return your good wishes, and will do as you bid. . . . We must do as he says, Crito . . . let the cup be brought, if the poison is prepared. . . .

The servant then handed the cup to Socrates, who . . . looking at the man with all his eyes, Echecrates, as his manner was, took the cup and said: What do you say about making a libation out of this cup to any god? May I or not?

The man answered: We only prepare, Socrates, just so much as we deem enough.

I understand, he said: Yet I may and must pray to the gods to prosper my journey from this to that other world . . .

Then holding the cup to his lips, quite readily and cheerfully he drank off the poison . . . But now when we saw . . . that he had finished the draft we could no longer forbear, and in spite of myself my tears were flowing fast;

so that I covered my face and wept . . . Nor was I the first. . . .

Socrates alone retained his calmness: What is this strange outcry? he said. . . .I have heard that a man should die in peace. Be quiet then, and have patience.[2]

This passage described an event, a happening, and a cup is part of that happening. Let us dwell upon the scene for a moment—the sunset, the approaching darkness, the cup of hemlock, the philosopher about to die, the group of friends lost in their grief. Holding the cup to his lips, Socrates drinks off the poison:

> Such was the end, Echecrates, of our friend . . . A man, as we may say, the best of all our time that we have known.[3]

We see the cup in action, playing a part.

A child, when he looks at this cup will say, "Cup, white, round, drink, mine!" A painter will say, "Here is a spot of white against a dark background." The scientist will say, "Here is a hollow china vessel made to drink out of." But the man of the theatre says, "Look at that cup! What's going to happen to it?!" And there you have the essence of the *art* of the theatre, the sense of happenings, the sense of occurings, the sense of occasions. To the artist of the theatre this object—and all objects, and all forms, and all events, and all actions—are a part of a vast drama that is being played out at this instant upon the stage of the world. But this is not all. In the theatre the cup is not only alive, it is *living*. I am talking of strange things now—eternal things. In the library, between the covers of a book, Hamlet is alive. But in the theatre, Hamlet is *living*. He has a body, nerves, a voice; and we hear him say:

> Here, thou incestuous, murderous, damned Dane,
> Drink off this potion.

You will observe that this is an unusual way of evaluating a play. Not at all the sort of thing we are accustomed to seeing in the dramatic departments of our newspapers. Not to ask whether a play is well directed, or well cast, or well set and costumed and lighted; but quite simply to ask: "Is it living?" Has it the power to quicken an audience into that nameless sense of life—so hard to describe, so easy to feel? The thrill of the nerves we experience when we hear Hamlet say:

> I'll observe his looks,
> I'll tent him to the quick. If he but blench,
> I know my course.

And it is brilliantly clear that measured by this measuring stick—I submit that this is the only valid way to measure a play—many of our current productions, even many of our biggest box office successes, have no more to do with the theatre than the busywork they give children in kindergartens.

But I did not come here to give you my opinion of contemporary show business. My purpose is simply to remind you, over and over again, that the art of the theatre is an art of awareness. This awareness, I call it "the theatre awareness," is what sets creators in the theatre apart from other people—a sense of living that is so strong it can make us feel that what we call living isn't living at all, but a kind of sleep. I am exceedingly anxious to be clear at this point. It is not enough to say that artists of the theatre have an unusual sense of life. All artists have an unusual sense of life. That is what makes them artists. But the peculiar "theatre sense of life" is the ability to sense the life that is in this instant and the next instant and the next—the raw, stinging, quick of living, as it rushes upon us out of the mysterious future and vanishes away from us forever into dreams. This sense of the instant, this "theatre awareness" of each instant as it flies away, is one of our rarest gifts, and one most boldly to be cherished. If you have it your life can be more wonderful than anything you have ever known. I want you to know that it can be full, that it can be rich, that it can be drunken with beauty and power. And that elation, exaltation—what the poet Steadman calls "the intensified feeling of man's being and becoming" can be your daily bread.

Realizing these things I want you to get a real sense of responsibility towards the theatre. And then I want you to throw out the trash—the trash in the theatre and the trash in your own thinking. Throw it out without pity, without mercy. I want you to learn that observation is not a substitute for insight. That ingenuity is not a substitute for imagination. That cleverness is not a substitute for culture. I want you to realize that America and Americans are not in the least like what we thought they were. To realize fully how deficient we are in a sense of reality, and how we try to compensate for it in all sorts of dazzling and futile ways. I want you to cherish a fierce, relentless belief in the greatness of this art to which you have dedicated yourselves. And then I want you to begin to create in the theatre out of a new awareness of ourselves and our country. Remembering always that it is an unforgivable thing to have small dreams—an unforgivable thing to have small dreams.

Now we come to the real question—the 64-dollar question. Assuming that what I have said, up to now, is in some measure true—Plato said, you know: "What I have said may not be true, but something very like it is true"—how does it affect you, and what are you going to do about it? The first thing, in my opinion, is to accept, once and for all, the fact that the theatre is an art. You will be surprised to learn how few people today consider the theatre seriously from the point of view of art. We may speak of the art of cookery, and the art of dressmaking, and even of the manly art of self-defense; but when we go so far as to speak of the theatre as an art, the image that comes most readily into the minds of most of us is the image

of a long-haired, and bedraggled, and dissolute old Thespian
mouthing scenes from long forgotten classics. The idea of the
theatre as an art, carrying with it the promise and the splendor
of art—yes, and the responsibility that goes with the practice
of art—is still a new and disturbing one to most of us. The first
thing then for us to realize is that the theatre is an art. And the
next thing to realize is that it is a backward art, stuck fast in
yesterday. We have no time to waste in sighing for vanished
glories. Our job is to build. But the plain truth is that our
theatre doesn't deal any longer, either in subject or in form,
with matters that really concern us. In other times and hours
the theatre may have reflected life, but it certainly does not
reflect the life of our time. Its approach has long since ceased
to keep pace with our thought. The outward behavior of the
characters our dramatists create may be up-to-date but what
goes on in their minds is very old-fashioned indeed. The mind
of an audience—its state of being, its capacity for experience—
is far, very far, ahead of what it sees on the stage. Someday an
audience is going to rise to its feet, en masse, during a performance and say, "Who do you think we are? What kind of people
to you take us for?" I hope *I* am in the theatre that night.

Of all the arts the theatre can least afford to be out of touch
with life. That is if it is to be a living theatre. But we are
working with stale concepts. The tools of our trade are all of
an old-fashioned make. We have no medium at hand with
which to express a contemporary situation in dramatic terms—
no contemporary medium, that is. This is true, I think, and it
is sad. For it means that the theatre has forgotten its audience.
It has taken liberties with its audience. The art of the theatre
is an art of feeling. The subject matter of the theatre is the
beating of the human heart and the human heart is very old.
The theatre deals with emotions—impulses, urges, drives, we
call them—all of them exceedingly ancient. They were felt by
the primeval worm before nature decreed that that worm
should twist off part of itself to make a head. They never

change. But, on the other hand, our way of expressing them does change. It changes from season to season, from generation to generation, from era to era; and that is our problem and our joy.

Our particular problem at the moment, it seems to me, is the fact that our theatre is so far from using the idiom of our own time. By idiom I do not mean merely the idiom of language. I mean, simply, that our way of expressing ourselves in the theatre is sadly behind the times—years and years. Part of our difficulty, it seems to me, lies in the fact that our conception of ourselves and the world we live in has changed so radically in recent years. For example, when Shakespeare made Hamlet say: "What a piece of work is a man!" he was speaking of a single exact entity. But this man:

> So noble in reason! So infinite in faculty in form and moving! So express and admirable in action! So like an angel in apprehension! So like a god![4]

this man has gone "boogie-woogie." And he goes riffin' up and down the land on the gin-mill special, blowin' big, fat, rat-bustin' notes on his trumpet and tappn' the tappa-hammer all the way from Memphis to St. Jo. He is a voice blared out over a public address system in baseball parks. He is a continent shuddering on a giant screen in a drive-in theatre mouthing the platitudes of Hollywood up there among the stars. He writes not with goose quill and ink horn on fair white parchment but in letters of smoke jetted from an airplane high overhead to advertise Pepsi-Cola or *The Outlaw*. His problems are solved for him by intricate electronic servo-mechanisms. He appears at the same instant on a thousand television screens. He moves from place to place at supersonic speeds. Under these strange new pressures new facets of the human psyche are being brought to light. Perhaps the human psyche itself is being altered by their impact. Who knows? Yet in our theatre there is hardly even a suspicion of their existence. And you know it as well as I do.

We get the impression from what we see in our theatres, and what we read in our newspapers, that the theatre is hardly worth bothering about—that it has long since ceased to be an exercise for adult minds. The opinion of the theatre is a discouraged one. We look in vain for aspiration, even for encouragement. The feeling is jaded and sorrowful. You're young. Make your choice now. Don't be satisfied with what you see in the theatre. Don't accept the counsels of a theatre that is dominated by the spirit of compromise. Don't accept what is offered you by frustrated, disillusioned, unhappy people. Don't let this be! Abandon a theatre whose natural condition is fear and move into a theatre whose natural condition is ecstasy. Realize that the theatre is incessantly changing, incessantly moving into something new, and fresh, and young. A theatre where it is always morning. And know that here is your only peace, your only joy, your only rest.

Let me tell you in conclusion the story that the actor, Hiram Sherman, told at a recent "pipe" night[5] at the Players Club. It seems that he was stationed at the Brooklyn Navy Yard at sometime during the late war. And when Christmas Eve came around, he was chosen to be Santa Claus and distribute presents. So he got ready. But just before he appeared, one of his superior officers suggested that a word of explanation might be in order before the ceremony began. Whereupon Hiram Sherman said:

"When they see me coming down the chimney, dressed in red, with a white beard, and a pack on my back; and when they remember what day it is, don't you think they'll know?"

Lecture 4

Curious and Profitable

N ot long ago in a collection of the prose writings of Walt Whitman I came upon a passage that gave me food for reflection:

> It would be a curious result, and a profitable one, to take a while to the theatre some man, highly educated and knowing the world in other things, but totally fresh to the stage; and let him give his real opinion of the queer sort of doing he would see there.

At the time he wrote these provocative words, Whitman was editor and dramatic critic of the *Brooklyn Daily Eagle*. Apparently he did not care a great deal for the theatre of McCready and Edwin Forrest and Junius Brutus Booth and the adored Jenny Lind. And yet in retrospect that theatre seems to us to have been a theatre of real social vitality. As I read I could not help wondering what Whitman would think of the theatre of our day, a hundred years later, if he could see it. He would be surprised, I felt, to say the least. Then I had a thought. Would it not be a curious and profitable result to take him at his word and introduce his ideal spectator for a time to the theatre we know. Such a man would find a "queer sort of doing there" no doubt. But I was sure that he would discover in what he saw some quality that spoke to him. Suppose one could put one's self into this attitude of mind. Suppose one could learn to look at the theatre for a moment from a fresh point of view—an absolute point of view—unhindered by the complicated problems of show business. It would be an original way to clarify one's ideas and one might arrive at some unexpected conclusions.

"Why not try it?", I said to myself. And I began to create in my imagination a hypothetical visitor: intelligent, educated, sensitive, worldly, and utterly ignorant of the theatre.

The process proved to be easier than I had anticipated. I repeated certain of the time-honored abracadabras of boyhood days consecrated to the evoking of familiar spirits. Tom Sawyer had taught them to me. And my guest appeared at once with an almost suspicious haste. Thereafter he became surprisingly articulate. So articulate, in fact, that I could have sworn he had been lurking in the neighborhood for some time waiting for this very opportunity to put in an appearance. I saw that his opinions were definite and that he had little hesitation in expressing them. He was refreshingly alert and eager and he could hardly wait for us to set out upon our tour of the various playhouses of the city. I began to look forward, with interest, to the experiment. The combination of general culture and particular ignorance was an intriguing one.

"Not every one," I said to myself, "is so fortunate as to have as a guest a man who has come all the way from Utopia."

But where should we begin? I was baffled for a moment. Then the Radio City Music Hall came to my mind—our biggest theatre, our most popular theatre, perhaps even our most representative theatre. Another murmured incantation—this one came straight out of *The Arabian Nights*—and we were seated in the mezzanine watching the great gold curtain loop lazily up and down. But I had not reckoned with my companion. To my amazement he was thoroughly unimpressed by the cavernous spaces of the showplace of the nation.

"I would rather see great dreams in a small place, than small dreams in a great place." he said, "It is an unforgivable thing to have small dreams."

"But this great place is America's very own dream." I said.

Then he remarked that our greatness sometimes seemed to him a matter of sheer bulk, rather than a matter of inner stature. And then he saw the Rockettes all lined up across the gigantic stage and kicking in unison, like the legs of a delirious mastodon centipede:

"Girls, and girls, and girls, and girls." he said, "But of course. Here is America's freedom. The freedom to do precisely what everybody else does. The freedom to be dominated by the idea of mass production. The freedom to decide not to be free. We will fight. We will die, if need be. For what? For the right to be regimented.

"This may be admirable," he said, "but it is certainly not very interesting. And, speaking for myself, I find it empty, and dreary, and very lonely. Precision dancers, the comfort of not being out of step. The consolation that lies in sameness. The danger of being an individual.

"An odd sign of the times." he mused as they rushed into the terrifying climax of their routine.

I lost no time putting an end to this particular experience. What had begun as a game was threatening to turn into something really serious. Perhaps it would be wiser to abandon the idea. But curiosity got the better of me.

"No," I said, "I will go on with it," and we continued our tour.

Then the fun began. I introduced my guest to every variety of theatrical entertainment the town could offer. I exposed him, so to speak, to every aspect of the contemporary theatre. It was exciting to see how quickly he caught on to the new medium of expression. After his preliminary queries had been answered regarding the arbitrary length of the plays he had seen, and their arbitrary division into acts and their disturbing intermissions—answered somewhat lamely and unconvincingly I must admit—we settled down to the business of playgoing. Very soon I ceased to feel the need of explaining to him the meaning of what went on behind the proscenium arch. Presently, there came a break in our routine. One evening, after dinner at the club, he began to talk of the things he had seen.

"By the terms of our agreement," he said, "I knew nothing of the art of the theatre when I began this experiment with you. But I saw at once that it is one of the great arts of the world— perhaps the greatest art of all because it is the most immediate. By contrast, the other arts seem to describe life, interpret life, illustrate life; whereas the art you have shown me is life itself. Before I could begin to feel at home in your theatre it was necessary for me to evolve for myself a concept of this art—so new and strange to me at first. If music could be called the art of the sound of life, I thought, if painting is the art of the look of life, if literature is the art of the recording of life, then the art of the theatre is the art of the living of life. All the sciences, all the other arts are teaching us about man's living. But drama *is* man's living. It is precisely this intimate association of art with life that makes the theatre so endlessly fascinating to me—life, transformed into art on the stage, before my eyes.

"What may be the tritest of commonplaces to you," he said, "came to me with the impact of a great discovery. Imagine, if you can, the delight, the excitement, the heady joy I felt at being brought face to face for the first time with an art whose idiom is life itself. I often recall the words of Whitman— through whose courtesy I am here—'I announce a life that shall be copious, vehement, spiritual, bold,' and each evening when the curtain rose on a new theatrical production my heart was filled with new eagerness.

"That was in the beginning." he said, "but as time went on I saw that your theatre is almost wholly lacking in the authority I am accustomed to associate with art. In spite of its brilliance, and its color, and its extraordinary mechanical proficiency; and in spite of the frantic ballyhoo that surrounds it—the theatrical sections of your Sunday papers deafen me and blind me—there is something profoundly unsure at the heart of it. It is plausible, and ingratiating, and even placating; but at the same time it is curiously tepid and jaded. The inner content is missing—the inner strength, the stamina. I do not sense the vitality of true artists at work. Your theatre is filled with uncertainty—weary in its inner feeling and sad. The life it presents behind the proscenium arch is something less than life—something undersized and dwarfish, a stunted theatre."

"You mean that the theatre reflects the insecurity and the uncertainty of the life of our time?" I asked.

"No." he answered, "the insecurity the theatre reflects is not the insecurity of the life that goes on around us, but an insecurity in the body of the theatre itself—an uncertainty as to its own nature and its own purposes. There is plenty of ingenuity there, and lots of novelty, and lots of experimentation, of a sort; but the plain truth is that it doesn't deal, either is subject or in form, with matters that really concern us. In other times than ours the theatre may have reflected life but it certainly does not reflect the life of our time. Its approach does not keep pace with our thought. The outward behavior of the characters your dramatists create may be up-to-date, but what goes on in their minds and their hearts is very old-fashioned indeed. The mind of audiences—their state of being, their capacity for experience—is far ahead of what they see on the stage. We are in the midst of bewildering breakdown of outworn conventions and a slow and painful growth of new ones. The world is moving, in agony, toward a new consciousness.

But, for some reason, your theatre reflects little of this ten-
sion—the horrifying 'unawareness' of life in the face of the
drama that is being played out on the front page of every
newspaper.

"Not long after I had the pleasure of making your acquaint-
ance," he said, "I came across a speech from one of your
dramas: 'What a piece of work is a man,' and the rest. That
speech lives in my memory:

> How noble in reason! How infinite in faculty! In form,
> in moving, how express and admirable! In action how like
> an angel! In apprehension how like a god!

I find there the praise of life without which art is nothing, 'a
sounding brass, a tinkling cymbal.'[1] But the speech was written
many years ago, I am told. I cannot escape the impression that
the writers and the producers and the actors and the directors
of your theatre have a low opinion of their fellow-men. They
have lost the sense of 'wonder.' They prefer the 'dim view.'
They ignore our hunger for nobility. They appear to have
entered into a conspiracy to behave as if there were no longer
any 'mystery' in human beings. That is what makes the inner
life of the characters in your plays so pitifully meager. You
oversimplify life. We are not so small or so petty as your
theatre makes us out to be. Is it the candid camera that has made
you so preoccupied with externals? Of all the arts your theatre
can least afford to be out of touch with life. That is, if it is to
be a living theatre. But you are working with stale concepts.
The tools of your trade are all of an old-fashioned make. At this
moment you are in real need of a way of presenting life in the
theatre that corresponds to our consciousness of ourselves—to
our patterns of thinking and feeling—a newer way, a fresher
way.

"But after all," he said, "the kind of theatre you have shown
me is a transitory thing. Its sun has set and what I have seen

is only an afterglow. The basic concepts of the theatre will change and the theatre of today will be as if it had never been. Once let a new convention of the theatre be adopted, once let America's restless enthusiasm take hold of it; and we shall see something very surprising indeed. I wonder what a new theatre would be like?" he said.

It was odd to hear the theatre spoken of in these ultimate terms—odd, and not altogether pleasant. Suddenly I remembered that my guest had never seen a motion picture. Here, perhaps, was the new theatre he was looking for. Again the murmured words—I was fast becoming an accomplished amateur magician in the Mark Twain manner—and we were watching the latest "super spectacle" of the cinema in an auditorium that reminded him now of Westminister Abbey, and now of the Alhambra, and now of the *Salle de Glasse* at Versailles. He was fascinated by the picture, as I knew he would be. But, to my surprise, he was even more fascinated by the audience. His eyes kept wandering from the screen to the rows of faces intent on the shifting images above them.

"How extraordinary!" he said again and again, "How extraordinary! I can hardly realize it. For the first time in history we have a medium that deals in pure thought. This screen drama we are watching is not a drama at all—it is a dream about a drama, a memory of a drama, the thought of a drama. And this newsreel. These are not the events. They are mental pictures of the events occurring after the events have taken place. But why does the audience accept these pictures as realities?

"Something very strange indeed has been happening to us here," he said, as we left the great picture palace. "For the past hour we have been dreaming. See the expressions on the faces of the people around us. They are waking out of a daydream. We know we are awake when we are awake, but we don't know we are dreaming when we are dreaming. This medium is a dream medium. The art of the motion picture is an art of reverie."

"Do you realize," I said, "that what you are saying goes contrary to the whole idea of motion pictures as they are being made?"

"It is so." he said obstinately. "These moving shadows we are seeing are not realities. They are only images of reality. This experience we are having is a subjective experience. How different our sensations are from our sensations in the theatre—as different as sleep from waking. There on the screen is the 'dreaming mind.' Let me see more!"

We set out on a second tour of the cinema theatres—more surprising, more disturbing than the first. We watched the pictures of the girl with the legs, and the girl with the bust and the look and the voice, and the he-man, (my companion wondered why no one ever spoke of a she-woman) and the ape-man swinging through the trees, and the sultry sirens, and the cowboys, and the hard-eyed killers, and the Mother Goose drawings that walked and talked and sang. At one point he interrupted our pilgrimage in the middle of a picture to rush to a theatre for a few moments and back again.

"It is as I thought," he said, dropping breathless into his seat. "There the experience is a communal one. The excitement is shared. Everyone in the audience is a part of it and everyone in the audience is awake and aware. But in this motion picture theatre our experience is solitary—not shared. The audience is an agglomeration, not an entity. Each of us here is alone, dreaming his own dream. And the strange thing is that although each of us dreams the dream separately, we are all dreaming the same dream—a Hollywood dream. The makers of these pictures have a terrible power put into their hands. They are canalizing our thought process. They are telling us what our desires and our motives and our aspirations shall be. Do they know what they are doing?"

"Yes." I said, "They know."

"It is obvious," he said, after a time, "that the makers of motion pictures think of them as theatre on an enormous popular scale—a kind of poor man's theatre. I sense a pathetic effort on their part to make these images real. But in trying to do this they are guilty of a serious error in thinking. Motion pictures, considered as theatre, can never be anything but a substitute theatre—an ersatz theatre. They lack the actuality that true theatre must have. These images can never be real. They are apparitions, emanations, part of the self sent forth at will. They can never pierce the veil. They can never be anything but dreams. They appear to us as dreams appear to us, and they haunt us as dreams haunt us. What an amazing thing would have happened if your picturemakers had realized from the very beginning that these images are, after all, only images; and that, instead of patterning their screen dramas after stage plays, they had written them in pure imagery—pure thought language—not deformed literature, not distorted painting—the thought stream itself running clear and free. Surely there is nothing far-fetched in recognizing the fact that the medium of the motion picture is a subjective medium and treating it frankly as such. The stream of consciousness method of writing is already a commonplace of literature. It will not be long before your writers will have learned to express themselves in pure thought on the screen. The secret lies in knowing that motion pictures are not real. How does it happen that you have not always known this?"

Here was something I had not bargained for. It seemed to me that my imaginary guest, with his unworldly pronouncements, was beginning to take on the attributes of a Frankenstein. A vivid memory came to my help—something I had once seen in one of George White's *Scandals*. Again I murmured the familiar incantations. We were seated in a theatre watching a vaudeville comedian on the stage as he sang a duet with his own image that sang from the screen behind him. *He* grew grave at once.

"I know now why I came," he said. "This is why I am here. This is what I came to see."

We were dining at the club for the last time and my visitor was giving me his final impression of the queer sort of doing he had seen in our theatre. I listened carefully for I knew I should not see him again. He spoke with great earnestness and sometimes his words seemed merely strange and sometimes there seemed to be something curiously prophetic about them.

"Your theatre is a very strange place," he said, "bewildering, filled with limitless possibilities, a fantastic place, a place to conjure in. But there is a curious discrepancy between life as we live it and life as we see it on the stage. I must confess that, up to now, I have been criticizing your dramatists for their failure to grasp the essence of life. But I have come to feel that the fault is not so much theirs as the fault of the idiom they are using. The theatrical forms of today can no longer communicate to us the tastes and pressures of the world. Life has passed them by. It has outgrown them as a healthy boy outgrows a suit of clothes. Now, suddenly, I have seen the suggestion of a new theatrical idiom that can really encompass the life of today. Here in this fragment from a forgotten musical comedy is the germ of a new theatre that is to be. A man sings to us and his inner self sings with him. Such a thing has never happened before in the history of the theatre. Why it should happen at this particular moment, I cannot say. The example before us is tiny, it is tentative, but it is alive. And it is pivotal. New forces converge upon it and radiate from it. There is a new promise in it.

"When I saw a living person and a motion picture on the stage at the same time," he said, "a curious thing happened. In relation to the person before it, the film becomes visible thought, visible emotion, visible thinking and feeling. The true subjective quality of the film became apparent at once. And now I see a new kind of theatre altogether—a new kind of drama, a new kind of acting, a new kind of presentation—a theatre with a promise of growth in in. A theatre embodying

all the eagerness of today—the restlessness, the reaching out
for new and vital forms of expression, a natural theatre, a
splendidly normal theatre—standing clear in what our friend
Whitman calls the 'flaunt of the sunshine.' "

"Tell me what it is you see." I said.

"At the root of all our living," he said, "is a consciousness
of our essential duality. That is our contribution to history—
the thing that gives measureless excitement to the life and the
thought of today. We are making a new beginning. We are
learning to add to actuality the power of the dream. And now
there is a way to say all this in the theatre—simply and easily,
straight and plain.

"Concretely," he said, "I see a motion picture placed on the
stage above and behind the actors. It is as simple as that. The
action of the play takes place against the background of a
motion picture which shows the unspoken thoughts and feelings of the characters. On the stage: their outer life; on the
screen: their inner life. The stage used objectively, the screen
used subjectively, in a kind of dramatic counterpoint. Not
motive as it is revealed in action, but action *and motive* simultaneously revealed to us. The simultaneous expression of the two
sides of our nature is an exact parallel to our life process. We
are living in two worlds at the same time—an outer world of
actuality and an inner world of vision. Day by day the inner
world is becoming clearer to us. The irrational side of ourselves—the unembodied part of ourselves—is being brought to
light. We are beginning to utter thought as thought, not
thought as speech; to utter feeling as feeling, not feeling as
speech. We are beginning to express thought and emotion
while they are happening to us, in their own idiom, before they
become translated into ordinary expression. We are beginning
to feel aloud and to think aloud. We are beginning to utter the
things that are unspoken as well as the things that are spoken.
And we are beginning to see that life, which is the subject

matter of all drama, is neither an expression of actuality nor an expression of vision, but an expression of the relation between the two.

"Life," he said, "is a never ending dialogue between the outer self and the inner self which together make up our dual nature. Every being has his own inner dream. Life as we see it today, is our relation to that dream—what we do to it, what it does to us, whether we listen to it or violate it. And it is the relation between life and the dream, between the dream and life, that is the subject matter of the new drama. There seems to be no way, as yet, to say this more clearly. Perhaps life, as we know it, is a perpetual dawning half-way between the life of the night and the life of the day. Perhaps it is like driving a tandem of horses—a white horse and a black horse. Perhaps it is like a journey along the seashore, with the familiar land on the one side and the mysterious ocean on the other. Our new awareness of both worlds is the fundamental characteristic of the life we are leading and it is the fundamental characteristic of the drama that is to be. It is strange, striking, that just at the very moment when the new concept of duality has come into being, a medium should be at hand by which it can be expressed in the theatre. Suppose someone were to find that he could help us to view the outward confusions and conflicts of today in a new light—the light of our inner drives. Suppose our most secret dreams were to be made visible and audible and we saw them influencing our lives and our lives influencing them. Will a new dramatist presently appear who can look outward at the life about him and inward at his own heart?"

I did not answer him. My mind was filled with strange imaginings. Did these far-flung ideas of his rest upon a foundation of truth? Could it be that a new, vivifying impulse is about to manifest itself in our theatre?

"Eeerrr . . . Yes." I said presently, "I see." He looked at me for a moment.

"Perhaps I am mistaken." he said, "Then this experience has been merely a harmless diversion. But perhaps I'm right. What then?"

He was gone.

Part Three

Reactions to the Lectures
and
The New Theatre
of Robert Edmond Jones

Reactions to the Lectures

J ones was available for lecture tours apparently from 1941 to 1952. Reports on the lectures are as sketchy as his itinerary. Press accounts of his speeches at various locations are generally brief or cursory, though some do give an insight into the dynamics of the event that featured his lecture. *The Minnesota Daily* for April 21, 1950, perhaps in an attempt to heighten the controversial aspects of Jones' lecture, headlined its coverage at the University of Minnesota the day before with: "Theatre Of Today Is Still a Backward Art—Jones".[1]

The Wooster Alumni Bulletin for June, 1950, noted that it was a "memorable year" for the Little Theatre on the campus of The College Of Wooster. And indeed it was. Not only did Thornton Wilder play the Stage Manager in *Our Town* there but "Another provocative evening came in the form of a lecture by Robert Edmond Jones, artist, designer, and producing manager."[2]

Occasional press reports provide a more candid glimpse into the reaction that Jones created when he spoke. In reporting on an informal talk to the Easy Chair and U-Players groups at the Playhouse on the campus of the University of Kansas City; *The University News* for April 6, 1949, noted that Jones

> said that the future of the American Theatre lies in groups such as we have here at the University, and "revolutionaries" who may come from these groups. The meeting came to a close no less than three times, each time beginning again as a result of a question or a remark from the audience which led Jones into a new train of thought. Members of the clubs were still arguing points of debate hours afterward.[3]

Some personal reactions to Jones' appearances also attest to the extraordinary nature of his lectures. Althea Hunt, Director of the Institute of the Theatre at the College Of William And Mary, in a letter to Mr. Robert Keedick of the Keedick Agency, noted about Jones's lecture on July 19, 1948, that;

> I can say without reservation that it was undoubtedly the most exciting and stimulating experience we have had this summer. Everyone was unanimous in expressing their delight and enthusiasm and even devotion to Mr. Jones. His subject matter was creative and thought-provoking, and his personality has charm and sincerity. He really is "the living theatre" about which he talks. Only superlatives can express our satisfactions in knowing him.[4]

This sense of the extraordinary that surrounded the visit of Jones to a group or a university campus is eloquently and humorously recounted in a gracious recollection from Professor Horace W. Robinson, Professor Emeritus of the University of Oregon at Eugene. In recounting his work as founder of and Executive Secretary and Program Director for the Northwest Drama Conference, he recalls that;

Our first conference in 1948 was quite successful so I decided to take a big plunge and wrote to Jones to see if he would come for 1949. At first he said it was not feasible, both in terms of time and money, but later he agreed that if he could have other West Coast lectures he would reconsider. As I recall it, the number agreed upon was four and eventually we lined up a total of four in February of that year. I believe all of the others were in California. He was to speak in Eugene first, on a topic of his own choice. I did not know until some time later that apparently he used the same material in these and later addresses. Upon arrival he had two very basic requests. (1) He wanted a bottle of scotch, which he discovered to his horror he could not purchase because Oregon sells liquor only through its own stores and at that time you had to have a resident permit to buy. Unfortunately, I did not have one either and could not buy for him so my wife prevailed on a friend to supply a bottle for the distinguished visitor. (2) He said his speech needed a single, very common, large, heavy, thick, round kitchen coffee cup, which was to be used as the illustrative focus for his remarks. I came up with a number of cups from home and from friends but none of them would do because they were too decorative, too fragile, too dainty, etc. Finally I went to a local hardware store and bought one of those old fashioned metal cups with baked on white enamel finish and a blue line trim. He was delighted with it— indicating that it was much better for his purposes than the one he had described. He fondled it, pointed to it, demonstrated with it for the entire period of his address, which was something less than an hour as I remember it. (I still have the cup—which has never been washed—and as a special reward I sometimes allow favored graduate students to take a sip of their selected beverage from it.)

A few minutes into the speech I suddenly realized with horror that I had made no arrangements to have the speech recorded. I knew Jones was not speaking from a prepared text as I had seen his rough notes and most of the presentation was extempore . . . But it was brilliant and all of the members of his audience knew that they were present on a memorable occasion. Jones himself seemed quite elated and I know that he used the same material for later speeches. James H. Ellingwood, a later scene designer at Oregon, told me that he knew about the speech and that it had been recorded on one of the later presentations but he could never recall who had the tape,

Unfortunately for Jones (but fortunately for me), there was a disruption of train service south—probably snow in northern California or a major wreck on the line—and his departure from Eugene was delayed for two days and we had several long talks and a tour around the countryside. He was much interested in my work in Western histori-cal pageantry and examined our materials in the ware-house with great care: covered wagons, stage-coaches, bull wheels, early hearses, etc. He was also fascinated by our Oriental Art Museum—one of the best in the coun-try—he had just come off *Lute Song*[5] and was saturated with Oriental art lore.

I remember one of our discussions turned on the sub-ject of the difficulty young theatre artists (playwrights, actors, designers, etc.) have in breaking into the profes-sional theatre with its deeply entrenched and older artists. He became quite aroused on the subject and I remember him jumping to his feet and beating on the table as he shouted "I sometimes think we all ought to *DIE* and just get out of the way!!"[6]

Clearly, Jones made a deep impression wherever he went. It would be fair to say that Gertrude Stein's statement—"The business of an artist is to be exciting"—was demonstrated fully when Jones spoke.

The New Theatre of
Robert Edmond Jones

From 1929 until his death on November 26, 1954, Robert Edmond Jones spoke and wrote of his vision of a "New Theatre." This theatre, as he saw it, was to be a synthesis of new technological developments, new philosophical and artistic perceptions, and the ancient art of the theatre.

By his own admission, there were precious few examples of this new theatre available for examination when he finally recorded his thoughts on it at Harvard in 1952. This, however, did not discourage him. Jones was confident his new theatre would emerge. Indeed, he said it was inevitable.

It is beginning to look as if he was right. A new sensibility has emerged in the theatre. It is irresponsible to suggest that this new sensibility is a direct result of contemporary artists' consciously implementing Jones's vision. That kind of linkage only happens in fiction, on the stage, or in the movies. But it is possible to affirm today that Jones was right in 1935 when he said, "These things will happen. They have to happen."[1] And that makes it useful to survey the development of Jones's vision and its present day manifestations.

The first record we have of Jones's vision of this new theatre comes in a contribution he made to the 1929 edition of the *Encyclopedia Britannica*. In an essay entitled, "Theory of Modern Production," Jones lays out his idea in preliminary form:

> In the simultaneous use of the living actor and the talking picture in the theatre there lies a wholly new theatrical art, an art whose possibilities are as infinite as those of speech itself.[2]

It is worth noting at this point that Jones wrote this in 1929 and *The Jazz Singer* had been released by Warner Brothers only two years before, in 1927. Thus, the world was still absorbing the fact of the "talkies" when Jones began to formulate his idea:

> ... that at this moment we have at our disposal a new and hitherto undeveloped medium of dramatic expression which during the next few years may profoundly change modern theatrical production. This medium is the talking picture.[3]

The experience of the talking picture was new, and Jones saw in it a way of giving fuller expression to a new movement in literature and art and drama, a movement attempting to give expression to the subconscious:

> Writers like James Joyce, painters like Matisse and Picasso, musicians like Debussy and Stravinsky, have ventured into the realm of the subjective and have recorded the results of their explorations in all sorts of new and arresting forms. Our playwrights, too, have begun to explore this land of dreams. In two dramas recently produced in New York, Eugene O'Neill's *Strange Interlude*

and Sophie Treadwell's *Machinal*, an attempt has been
made to express directly to the audience the unspoken
thoughts of the characters, to show us not only their
conscious behavior but the actual pattern of their subconscious lives.

The dramatists of today are casting about for ways in
which to express the working of the subconscious, to
express thought before it becomes articulate. They have
not seen the moving and talking picture is itself a
direct expression of thought before thought becomes articulate. They are trying to give us in the theatre not only
the outward actuality of our lives, but the inward reality
of our thoughts. They are seeking to go beyond the everyday life we normally know into the never-ending
stream of images which has its source in the depths of the
self, in the unknown springs of our being. But in their
search for ways in which to express their new awareness
of life, they have not observed that the moving picture is
thought made visible.

. . . Some new playwright will presently set a motion
picture screen on the stage above and behind his living
actors and will reveal the two worlds that together make
up the world we live in—the outer world and the inner
world, the world of actuality and the world of dream.[4]

The vision of this new theatre remained with Jones in the
succeeding years. His commitment to it deepened when, in
1934, he was hired by RKO to design sets and costumes for the
first color motion picture—*La Cucaracha*. Following this experience he wrote an article, "My Hollywood," for the October
1934 issue of *Vanity Fair*, in which he spelled out in more detail
his vision of what motion pictures are:

When we go to the theatre we see real people on the
stage, people of flesh and blood. But actors on the screen

are, of course, not real people at all. They are not even pictures, in the sense in which a photograph reproduced in the pages of this periodical is a picture. The fact that they move and speak makes them something else. Translated through this new medium, they become, not pictures, but images. We see them, not objectively as we might see the same actors in the theatre, but subjectively as Hamlet saw his father, in our mind's eye. These great beautiful images up there on the screen, those heroic breathing abstractions whose eyelashes we count, whose tresses gleam hyacinthine, whose perfect teeth loom over us, larger than the Radio City Tower, are not actual people at all. They are living ideals, living idols. Unreal, intangible as they are, they have in some curious way the power to dominate and enthrall our imaginations as no flesh and blood actors could ever enthrall them.[5]

What the difference is between film and theatre:

Motion pictures are no more like theatre than a concert is like a banquet. For we are dealing here, not with drama, but with pure myth. Performance, as we know it in the theatre, has no place here. Our conscious, critical faculties leave us. Reverence, curiosity, adoration crowd our minds.[6]

And what films could become:

This legendary glamour, this quality of myth is what I have found in Hollywood. Underneath its unreal, iridescent, chameleon-like exterior is this amazing core of truth. No one here in New York seems to realize it. But no matter what new stars are discovered, no matter what new stories are written, this thing I am writing about has always been true and will always be true. These people are hedged around with a lot of nonsense that is strange and unreal and depressing. And yet, somehow, in spite of all this, they are lifted up by some unknown magical law into another field of being. When will the rulers of motion pictures have the vision and the courage to move forward strongly into this new idea? Suppose they gave Greta Garbo great emotions, really great emotions, to interpret on the screen. Suppose the hidden spark that is in Katharine Hepburn really caught fire. Or suppose Clark Gable could become a symbol, not merely of the tender brutality of the bedchamber, but a symbol of everything a man can be in this world. Suppose, working together, they all gave us the sense of refreshment and power and faith that Toscanini gives us in his concerts.[7]

Jones continued his association with RKO into 1935, when he served as art director for the first feature length film in Technicolor, *Becky Sharp*. In June of 1935, *Becky Sharp* opened at the Radio City Music Hall and *Vanity Fair* featured an article by Jones entitled "A Revolution In The Movies." While this article was almost completely concerned with the problem and potential of color in motion pictures, there does appear one provocative paragraph in which Jones amplified his vision and insists on its inevitability.

The advent of color in pictures, it seems to me, is only the next step in an inevitable law of growth. First, there were black and white images of ourselves preserved in our family albums. Then, miraculously, these images began to move on a screen before us. Then they began to speak. Now they are taking on all the colors of life. Soon they are going to come to you in your own homes. Presently they will step off the screen and appear before you in the round—all but living. These things will happen. They

have to happen. They are all a part of our raging modern
thirst for discovery.[8]

Later, in August of 1935, Jones expanded his *Vanity Fair*
statement. In his contribution to the 25th Anniversary Postbag
of the *Yale Review*, he noted that:

The theatre twenty years from now will be no more like
the theatre of 1935 than *The Front Page* is like *Everyman*
or the Radio City Music Hall is like an Elizabethan inn-
yard. It will be conditioned by the cinema, by television,
by other mechanical inventions undreamed of as yet, conditioned most of all, by the vast changes in society which
it mirrors.[9]

Clearly, as this quote shows, Jones's vision of the new theatre
was one which would exploit all the latest in contemporary
technology. But, it would not merely make use of new technology. Jones saw clearly in 1935 what we still have difficulty
understanding today. He realized that technology is only the
physical manifestation of deeper changes that occur in society,
and he saw that the use of this technology is a key to assist our
understanding of these societal changes. Indeed, if one theme
is truly consistent in the thoughts of Jones, it is just this: that
"the business of workers in the theatre is . . . to express a
timeless theme by means of the tools of one's own time."[10]
Unfortunately, Jones's association with motion pictures was
severely limited from this time on. The only other film he
worked on, *Dancing Pirate*, was released by RKO in 1936. But
if he made no more films, his interest in the aesthetic problems
of film and the relationship of film to theatre remained. His
reflections and speculations continued for the next five years.
It is probable that during this time Jones wrote and privately

circulated his essay, "Curious and Profitable," which contained more thoughts on this subject.

Jones returned to his theme with the publication of *The Dramatic Imagination* in 1941. In the opening chapter of the book, Jones went back to his thoughts of 1929 and restated his belief that this fusion of film and live theatre was to become the theatre of the future. Again he expresses his sense of the inevitability of this occurrence.

> All art moves inevitable toward this new synthesis of actuality and dream. Our present forms of drama and theatre are not adequate to express our newly enlarged consciousness of life. But within the next decade a new dimension may be added to them, and the eternal subject of drama—the conflict of Man and his Destiny—will take on a new significance.[11]

But Jones now expanded his ideas further. He now perceived that the motion pictures had a new power. That power is the ability to present reality and to become a liberating force for the theatre:

> Motion pictures naturally attract to themselves everything that is factual, objective, explicit. Audiences are gradually coming to prefer realism on the screen to realism in the theatre. Almost insensibly Hollywood has brought an irresistible pressure to bear upon the realistic theatre and the picture frame stage. Future generations may find it hard to believe that such things ever existed. ... Motion pictures are about to become a great liberating agent of drama. By draining theatre of its literalness they are giving it back to imagination again.[12]

All the threads were finally in place and Jones tied them all together into a complete statement of his vision of this new theatre when he embarked upon his lecture tour in 1941. Promotional literature advertising his tour said that he was prepared to speak on three subjects "The Theatre of the Future," "The Art of the Theatre," and "Why We Have Theatres." For the next several years, Jones toured the country speaking at colleges, universities, and at other gatherings concerned with the arts in America. Speaking sometimes from typed manuscripts, sometimes from rough notes, and sometimes extempore,[13] Jones developed his themes and his vision of the new theatre.

At one such meeting, a symposium entitled, "Drama And The Other Arts," held at the Metropolitan Museum on January 21, 1943, Jones delivered a speech, "The Drama of the Future." As we have noted, this was a recast and retitled version of his lecture tour speech, "The Theatre of the Future."

Here is the first record we have, in the clearest possible terms, of Jones's vision of this new synthesis of film and live theatre. The vision was complete and we know precisely what Jones had in mind as this extended quote from the manuscript shows:

> . . . Presently some new dramatist will see that the subjective experience can be most clearly and truthfully expressed by means of the motion picture, and the characters of his drama will appear simultaneously on the stage and on the screen, living their outward and inward lives before us at the same time. This is the new drama I forsee.
>
> For the sake of added clearness I will restate in the simplest possible terms what I have said so far. I believe:
>
> That our contemporary drama still deals, for the most part, with objective experience.
>
> That this objective approach is the result of a photographic habit of mind which in turn is closely linked with the development of the camera.
>
> That photographs have begun to move and speak and

that in doing so they have ceased to be an objective experience and have become subjective experience.

That our painters and our novelists and certain of our dramatists have begun to explore the subconscious element in ourselves and to express it directly in its own character, before it becomes translated into action.

That the motion picture is the ideal medium with which to interpret our subconscious experience.

And that the drama of the future will deal, not with objective experience or subjective experience, but with both varieties of experience at the same time, expressing our essential duality in a new theatrical idiom involving the simultaneous use of the stage and the screen.

The facts at our disposal seem to me to point to this conclusion with inescapable logic. What follows is pure speculation. I am speaking of a drama and a theatre which do not yet exist. Only a poet could do the subject justice. The new drama will display, not only action, but the thought which prompts the action: not only the deed, but the emotion behind the deed. We shall see a continuous play and interplay between outward action and interior motive—the warp and woof of a new fabric. And for the first time in the history of the drama we shall see ourselves presented in our new wholeness, which we are only just beginning to understand.

The new drama—I might borrow a current expression and call it the "two-way" drama—will be presented on what I might call in turn a "two-way" stage. Objective experience will be interpreted by flesh-and-blood actors appearing on a stage which will resemble more or less closely the realistic stage we are familiar with today. But above and behind and around this stage a motion picture screen will be erected, and on it are thrown the shadow-selves of the characters of the drama, living and moving as thoughts and emotions live and move. Our attention is focused, now on the stage, now on the screen, now on both stage and screen, as the drama dwells upon outward or inward experience, or upon outward and inward experience at the same time . . . How shall I tell you? How can I evoke this for you? The images of the three weird sisters hover and scream above Macbeth and Banquo as they pause at the crossroads on the blasted heath:

> Flapping from out their Condor wings
> Invisible woe!

then making themselves air, into which they vanish. They manifest themselves, out of the icy fear which hangs over the banquet scene, inducing, as it were, the apparition of Banquo on the stage below them. The tragedy of RICH-ARD III unrolls its hideous tapestry beneath a sky of madness, stabbed through with violent images of crowns that drip blood, and enormous heraldic white roses, and murdered princes and kings and queens, wrapped in their winding-sheets. The spirit of Hamlet's father, "unhouseled, disappointed, unaneled," appears again and again throughout the play, a nervous excitation in Hamlet's mind. In the final scene the body of Hamlet is borne like a soldier to the platform. The stage darkens, is blotted out. The last peal of ordnance is shot off. Only a clear, still sky remains, a winter night in Elsinore. A star falls.

Now a scene from a drama of our own time. We see a high blank stone wall. Against it stands a man, blindfolded and manacled. Across from him, a firing squad. The order is given to present arms. The soldiers raise their rifles. There is a pause. The stage grows dim. On the screen above a spot of vivid light writes a monstrous enlargement of the doomed man's cardiagraph, the spasmodic, furious beating of his heart. Another: on the stage we see the interior of a peasant's cottage somewhere in Central Europe. Lamplight. Firelight. Father and Mother

talk to their children, quietly, in low voices, soothing
them, saying unimportant things. Above them, around
them, blurred and vague, the shadows of Nazi armies
marching. Lidice . . .

These foreshadowings are only the faintest and most
halting intimations of what we may expect to see in the
theatre when the new dramatist takes his material in hand
and begins to make his great orchestrations of the seen
and the unseen.[14]

It is important to note than Jones's vision was of nothing
more or less than a completely new form of theatre. It was, as
he envisioned it, to be a technological *and* philosophical synthesis that would give dramatic expression to the condition of
contemporary man. It is this condition, this realization of the
relationship between our outer and inner lives, that Jones
sought to reconcile with his new drama and his new theatre.
This reconciliation, as Jones defined it from his prophetic and
humanistic perspective, is actually a process of healing. At the
end of his presentation he said:

> . . . We hear a great deal today about the coming
> Century of the Common Man. Presently, it is true, our
> outward life will be fuller and more abundant than any-
> thing we have ever dreamed. But the new Century of the
> Common Man is actually the century of the common
> man's awakening into the mystery and the terror and the
> wonder of his own inner self. This is the way life is
> moving. We cannot hasten it or hinder it or alter it. It is
> a trend of the times, a part of the drift of history. Vistas
> of power open before us. We are turning inward, and in
> so doing we are finding out how much of us lives. We are
> finding out that we are not so small or so petty or so
> various or so mean as we seem to be. We know very little
> of the shadow-side of ourselves as yet, but we know

enough to know that the old gods dwell there, and the devils, and the daemons, the forces that shape our fate, our destiny, our horoscope. The new dramatist, like Prometheus, will bring to light "those fiery shapes that were aforetime wrapped in darkness." And on his stage he will give us a new conception of what life means—Man in relation to his own inner consciousness.

For it is not our outer life alone that has meaning for us today, nor our inner life alone, but the living relationship between our outer life and our inner life. And it is precisely this living relationship that is the subject of the new drama. In life as we live it our inner experience runs parallel to our outer experience but seldom meets it. The two varieties of experience are rarely fused. But the new drama will present to us, not only our life in relation to the world we live in, but our relation to our own inner dream. Here is its promise. Seeing it—hearing it—experiencing it we can become whole once more.[15]

From 1943 to his death in 1954 this remained Jones's statement on his view of the "New Theatre" even though, as he noted in the recording made at Harvard, "We shall not find many suggestions of this new synthesis in our playhouses in this Year of Our Lord, 1952."[16] And, so, the question can be fairly asked: "What suggestions of this new synthesis shall we find in our playhouses in this Year of Our Lord, 1991?" The answer is different depending upon where you look.

Unfortunately, the vast majority of theatre in the United States—that large, ongoing, unorganized confederation of theatres, both amateur and professional, that are dedicated to realism—has nothing whatsoever to do with Jones's New Theatre. For this confederation the movies did not, as Jones believed, draw realism out of the theatre. In fact, the reverse happened. The influence of motion pictures and television on this theatrical sensibility only accentuated the desire for a heightened realism in the theatre. There is in the American theatre a strong, powerful, and innate craving for the realistic, prosaic, and pedestrian recreation and representation. This natural craving and tendency was only fanned by the advent of movies because the movies, also, made a crucial error of perception at the beginning of their development, according to Jones:

> . . . the makers of motion pictures think of them as theatre on an enormous popular scale—a kind of poor man's theatre. I sense a pathetic effort on their part to make these images real. But in trying to do this they are guilty of a serious error in thinking. Motion pictures, considered as theatre, can never be anything but a substitute theatre—an ersatz theatre. They lack the actuality that true theatre must have. These images can never be real. They are apparitions, emanations, part of the self sent forth at will. They can never pierce the veil. They can never be anything but dreams. They appear to us as dreams appear to us, and they haunt us as dreams haunt us. What an amazing thing would have happened if your picture makers had realized from the very beginning that these images are, after all, only images; and that, instead of patterning their screen dramas after stage plays, they had written them in pure imagery—pure thought language—not deformed literature, not distorted painting—the thought stream itself running clear and free. Surely there is nothing farfetched in recognizing the fact that the medium of the motion picture is a subjective medium and treating it frankly as such. The stream of consciousness method of writing is already a commonplace of literature, It will not be long before your writers will have learned to express themselves in pure thought on the screen. The secret lies in knowing that motion pictures are not real. How does it happen that you have not always known this?[17]

Well, we still don't know why we didn't always know that. We also still don't know why we can't shake our stubborn addiction to realism in the theatre. Perhaps the problem is as basic and fundamental as Jones said it was:

> . . . Realism in the theatre is an infallible sign of low vitality. Just as elaborate scenic productions are an infallible sign of low vitality in the theatre. Realism is something we practice when we aren't feeling very well.[18]

Fortunately, there are areas in the American theatre where the picture is brighter and the feeling is better. Even though it has taken more time than Jones envisioned, certain courageous artists in our own country have ventured into this New Theatre.

Working out of what used to be called the avant-garde in the American theatre, individual artists and groups such as John Jesurun, Robert Wilson, Laurie Anderson, Ping Chong, the Wooster Group, Squat Theatre, Mabou Mines, and a host of performance artists and rock groups are exploring this synthesis with sometimes arresting results. Film, television, and live action sequences are mixed and presented in stage productions. A description of some recent productions provides the following examples:

> A play called "Dreamland Burns," by the Squat Theatre, begins with a 40-minute film projected on a screen at the front of the stage. When the main character falls asleep and dreams of a fire, real flames become visible through a screen—which then rises out of sight, revealing a stage crowded with props and characters for the second part of the show.
>
> In the first section of "The Road To Immortality," a trilogy by the Wooster Group, two visions of American life are boldly contrasted. On stage, live performers have

a nightmarish party in a surreal parody of a suburban
house. On video monitors above, the same performers do
scenes from a Thornton Wilder play in the style of a soap
opera. Later, a grainy 8mm film also flickers obscurely on
a broken-down TV set.

A play called "Deep Sleep," by John Jesurun, has two
groups of characters—one played by live performers, the
other seen as images on a movie screen. The groups
argue, each insisting that it's more "real" than the other.
Eventually some characters try to trade places, with tragi-
comic results.

Mabou Mines director Ruth Malezceck litters the stage
with movie screens of different shapes and sizes in
"Wrong Guys," a wry play about gangsters. Live and
filmed images overlap and intersect throughout the evening, to dizzying effect.[19]

Approaching their art from a post-modern sensibility, these
artists "are keenly aware of the need to appeal to a broader
based audience if they are to be heard, and welcome the challenge. 'Crossover' and 'Mainstream' are no longer dirty words,
but instead represent eventual goals."[20] And so this new synthesis is explored with the aim of attracting corporate sponsorship and a larger audience.

This "institutionalization" or "gentrification" of the avant-
garde springs from if not a new at least a refreshing perception
of the relationship of the artist to the audience.[21] These artists

> . . . are acutely aware of the demands of living in a media-
> saturated world. Whatever they may feel about that fact,
> they are determined to take advantage and express them-
> selves. If they incite, offend, or provoke us, it is in order
> to communicate, to establish a dialogue, and engage us in
> debate perhaps only with ourselves. It is a sign of respect
> for their (potential) audiences.

As Jesurun says, "A decade ago the idea about a mass audience was that they were stupid. It was the old art school mentality." No longer. Today's artists expect us to be able to form our own opinions. After all, we are always free to close our eyes. Or change the channel.[22]

This is a widely held perception. As playwright Robert Coe, who has collaborated with both Philip Glass and Laurie Anderson, noted:

> . . . avant-garde performing arts just don't play by the same rules as a decade ago . . . For the first time in the history of postwar experimental performance, serious artists have ceased to assume an attitude of indifference or superiority to the culture at large.[23]

And David Byrne observes:

> In the past, traditional artists didn't care what the public thought. More recently people want to show their stuff to a wider audience. People like Anderson and Glass don't consider it selling out to approach a popular audience.[24]

And Michael Walsh and Jeanne McDowell, in a recent *Time* Magazine article on the avant-garde in Manhattan noted that:

> In fact, the very rules of the game have changed, thanks to technology. The postwar transistor and video generations have grown up accepting the electronic media as legitimate sources of art. The late pianist Glenn Gould was considered odd when he abandoned the concert hall for the recording studio, but to the rock generation there is little or no difference between stereo loudspeakers and a live performance. The first group of performers who

have fully integrated technology into their acts have encountered listeners eager to celebrate their message.[25]

Jones would have understood and applauded this sensibility
and these efforts. Jones never viewed the theatre as a closed,
elite art form appealing only to rarefied and cultivated sensibili-
ties. After all, his own awareness of the capabilities of the
audience and the disservice done to it by the theatre of his day
prompted him to make this observation.

> . . . But the plain truth is that our theatre doesn't deal
> any longer, either in subject or in form, with matters that
> really concern us. In other times and hours the theatre
> may have reflected life, but it certainly does not reflect the
> life of our time. Its approach has long since ceased to keep
> pace with our thought. The outward behavior of the
> characters our dramatists create may be up-to-date but
> what goes on in their minds is very old-fashioned indeed.
> The mind of an audience—its state of being, its capacity
> for experience—is far, very far, ahead of what it sees on
> the stage. Someday an audience is going to rise to its feet
> en masse, during a performance and say, "Who do you
> think we are? What kind of people do you take us for?"
> I hope I am in the theatre that night.
>   Of all the arts the theatre can least afford to be out of
> touch with life. That is if it is to be a living theatre. But
> we are working with stale concepts. The tools of our
> trade are all of an old-fashioned make. We have no me-
> dium at hand with which to express a contemporary situ-
> ation in dramatic terms—no contemporary medium, that
> is. This is true, I think, and it is sad. For it means that the
> theatre has forgotten its audience. It has taken liberties
> with its audience.[26]

And to pose this interesting dilemma.

What a pity that the excitement that should be in the theatre should be found only in baseball parks, and arenas, and stadiums, and race courses.[27]

In our own time and in our own country, contemporary media are being employed in the dramatic expression of contemporary situations by artists who seek to communicate with a wide, popular audience. That is cause for celebration.

Meanwhile, a more complete example of Jones's new theatre exists. The Laterna Magika in Prague represents a fully developed example of his vision. Originally developed by Josef Svoboda and Alfred Radok for the Brussels Fair of 1958, the form owes its evolution to the prior development of Polyekran by Svoboda and Radok for that same fair and the pioneering earlier work by E. F. Burian with a form called Theatergraph. Laterna Magika enjoyed spectacular success in Brussels in 1958 and was given a permanent home in a converted motion picture theatre in Prague in 1959. However, artistic and political disagreements about the uses of the form hampered its development and Svoboda withdrew from it for some time.[28]

In 1973, new artistic efforts were possible in the theatre and with the presentation of *The Wonderful Circus* in 1977, a new creative team had been assembled, headed by Svoboda. Much experimentation and presentation has followed from this revitalization, and two new developments are worth noting specifically.

The first development was conditioned by the desire on the part of the creative team to fully explore and exploit all the possibilities of the medium and achieve the complete integration of film and theatre. Svoboda's comments on this are especially pertinent.

The play of the actors cannot exist without the film, and vice versa—they become one thing. One is not the background for the other; instead you have a simultaneity, a

synthesis and fusion of actors and projection . . . The film
has a dramatic function.[29]

Accordingly, the artistic thrust of Laterna Magika since 1977
has been to develop works written especially for it. In this way
the artists seek to counter the criticism, left over from the
earlier uses of the form, that it is only suitable for revue, caba-
ret, or tourist-type entertainment. Indeed, presentations since
1977 such as *The Wonderful Circus* and *One Day in Prague* have
deliberately appealed to the widest possible audience. But, in
addition to this, presentations such as *The Night Rehearsal, The
Talkative Snail,* and *The Black Monk* have expanded and explored the potentials of the medium. *The Night Rehearsal* (1981)
was the first drama presented on the Laterna Magika stage. It
featured the use of television and was meant primarily for
Czech audiences. *The Talkative Snail* (1983) is an opera in-
tended primarily for children. But of these three, the most
significant of the recent offerings is *The Black Monk*. Based on
a short story by Chekhov and dramatized especially for Laterna
Magika, the presentation opened in Prague in 1983 to great
success. In 1986 the production was recreated at the Hillberry
Theatre, Wayne State University, with an American cast. This
presentation offered American audiences the first exposure to
Laterna Magika in their own language.

In *The Black Monk*, film, lighting, settings, costumes, live
action, dialogue, direction, sound, and music are all welded
into an arresting theatrical experience capable of abrupt cuts,
slow elegiac transitions, montage, and juxtapositions. *The Black
Monk* also employs and intermingles multiple dramatic styles.
Now impressionistic, now symbolic, now realistic, the performance surges along a strong narrative line that explores the
themes of infatuation, love, obsession, happiness, the nature of
artistic talent, and individual isolation. The synergistic effect
of live performance and film expands our consciousness and,
for the audience member who comes with a mind free of

preconceptions and who is willing to accept the demands that the form imposes, reveals depths and facets of emotion, thought, and experience not possible in film or drama alone.

The second development is the fully detailed proposal by Svoboda and his collaborators for a new theatre to house Laterna Magika. The adaptation of the Adria Cinema Theatre in Prague in 1959 was not a perfect solution. The old cinema theatre imposed severe physical restrictions on the staging and artistic development of the form with the result that the live play was performed essentially on the stage apron and the film was projected into the space behind. This unsuitable situation retarded experimentation and meant that whatever fruitful development occurred came about ". . . only with the greatest difficulty, and always at the price of bitter artistic concessions."[30] The new studio has been designed to foster experimentation and make it possible for the creative team to develop the form still further. The aesthetic that informs the work of Laterna Magika in the 1980's reflects the same concerns and desires that Jones articulated in the 1940's.

. . . for Laterna Magika, the principles that attract most and are the most interesting are those that expand dramaturgic possibilities, those instances where the medium of Laterna Magika functions as the bearer of content and creates, in the interaction of stage and projection forms, quite new meaning and artistic dimensions.[31]

The "New Theatre" Robert Edmond Jones foresaw in 1929 has come into existence. In some instances it is still in a tentative, exploratory, experimental form. In other instances, it has developed into a mature expression. And in still other instances, the idea is so sophisticated that it is influencing theatre architecture and generating new proposals for experimental studio space.

It is an interesting experience to contemplate the above. The validity of Jones's vision exhilarates and inspires us in its multi-ple manifestations on the stages of the world today. Yet that exhilaration is tinged with sadness when one realizes it has taken approximately a half a century for the new synthesis Jones foresaw to become fully visible.

Even so, Jones's poetic vision of this new theatre was strong enough to sustain him throughout his life. In 1941 he wrote, "Out of the manifold contacts of my experience the image of a new theatre has gradually formed itself, a theatre not yet made with hands. I look forward to this ideal theatre and work toward it."[32] What new possibilities, we wonder, would he see in this theatre now? A more important question, however, is: What will we?

Notes

Introduction

1 Ralph Pendleton, *The Theatre of Robert Edmond Jones,* (Middletown, CT: Wesleyan University Press, 1959) p. 178.
2 Pendleton, p. 178. Pendleton identifies the following colleges and universities as being visited by Jones from 1941 on: Brooklyn Institute of Arts and Sciences, Carleton College, Carnegie Institute of Technology, University of Connecticut, Cornell College, Drake University, Fordham University, Iowa State College, University of Kansas City, MacMurray College, University of Minnesota, North Dakota State College, University of Oregon, Stanford University, University of Virginia, Wesleyan University, College of William and Mary, College of Wooster, Yale University.
3 Pendleton, p. 178.
4 Pendleton, p. 178.

Lecture 1

1 William Shakespeare, *Hamlet*
2 William Congreve, *The Way Of The World*
3 George S. Kauffman, *The Man Who Came To Dinner*
4 Clare Booth Luce, *The Women*
5 Henrik Ibsen, *The Lady from the Sea*
6 Maurice Maeterlinck, *Pelléas and Melisande*
7 William Butler Yeats, *The Shadowy Waters*
8 James Joyce, *Ulysses*
9 Anna Cora Mowatt Ritchie, *Fashion*
10 This is not a line from *Macbeth*, although it seems that it should be. It is from "Ligeia" by Edgar Allan Poe.

Lecture 2

1 The Old Vic production that appeared on Braodway in 1946.
2 A play by James Gow and Arnaud d'Usseau, produced on Broadway in 1946.
3 William Shakespeare, *Othello*
4 William Shakespeare, *Antony And Cleopatra*
5 William Shakespeare, *Romeo And Juliet*

Lecture 3

1 At this point in the recording, Jones coughed twice to indicate the stale quality of his previous statement.
2 Plato, *Phaedo*
3 Ibid.
4 The speech is transcribed as Jones said it, possibly from memory. The actual lines are:
    How noble in reason! How infinite in faculty! In form, in moving, how express and admirable! In action how like an angel! In apprehension how like a god!
5 The recording is unintelligible at this point. Jones may have said "pipe" night or "pump" night or some other variation.

Lecture 4

1 1 Corinthians, 13, verse 1
    Though I speak with the tongues of men and of angels, and have not charity, I am become as sounding brass, or a tinkling cymbal.

Reactions to the Lectures

1 *The Minnesota Daily*, April 21, 1950, Vol. LXX, No. III, Courtesy of University Archives, University of Minnesota.
2 *The Wooster Alumni Bulletin*, June, 1950, Courtesy of Andrews Library, The College of Wooster.
3 *The University News*, April 6, 1949, p. 4, Courtesy of University Archives, University of Missouri-Kansas City.
4 Letter from Althea Hunt to Robert Keedick, July 27, 1948, Courtesy of College Archives, The College of William and Mary.
5 A musical produced on Broadway in 1946.
6 Letter from Professor Horace Robinson to Delbert Unruh, May 6, 1983.

The New Theatre of Robert Edmond Jones

1 Robert Edmond Jones, "A Revolution in the Movies," *Vanity Fair*, June 1935: 13.
2 Robert Edmond Jones, "Theory of Modern Production," Encyclopedia Brittanica, 14 ed. (1929) 40.
3 Jones, "Theory" 40.
4 Jones, "Theory" 39–40.
5 Robert Edmond Jones, "My Hollywood," *Vanity Fair*, October 1934: 37.
6 Jones, "Hollywood" 37.
7 Jones, "Hollywood" 64.
8 Jones, "Revolution" 13.
9 Robert Edmond Jones, "The Anniversary Postbag," *Yale Review*, Autumn 1935: 22–23.
10 Robert Edmond Jones, *Towards A New Theatre*, Vocarium Records, 1955.
11 Robert Edmond Jones, *The Dramatic Imagination* (New York: Theatre Arts Books, 1941) 19.
12 Jones, *Imagination:* 132–134.
13 Personal recollection of Jones' lecture at the University of Oregon, Eugene, Oregon, 1949, by Prof. Horace W. Robinson.
14 Robert Edmond Jones, "The Drama of the Future," ms, Beinecke Library, Yale University: 19–22.
15 Jones, "Drama of the Future" 22–23.
16 Jones, "Towards A New Theatre."
17 Robert Edmond Jones, "Curious and Profitable," Vocarium Records, 1963. This lecture, based on the privately printed and circulated essay of the same name, is in the form of an extended conversation between Jones and a visitor he has constructed in his imagination who is well educated, but knows nothing of the theatre. Jones takes this visitor to all forms of theatre and then talks to him about his impressions.
18 Jones, "Towards A New Theatre."
19 David Sterritt, "Film and Video Joining Actors in Stage Works," *The Christian Science Monitor*, Monday, May 18, 1987: 23.
20 Jordan Simon, "The Gentrification of Avant-garde Theatre," *Taxi*, April 1987: 150.
21 The term "institutionalization" and the term "gentrification" are used by Arnold Aronson and Jordan Simon, respectively, to describe the process by which the avant-garde has sought wider audiences and corporate sponsorship. Simon's thoughts on the subject appear in the article cited above. Aronson's thoughts appear in: Arnold Aronson,

"Design and the Next Wave," *Theatre Design and Technology*,
Spring 1986: 8.

22 Simon 156.

23 Michael Walsh and Jeanne McDowell, "North of Dallas South of Hous-
ton, *Time*, October 27, 1986: 88.

24 Walsh and McDowell 88.

25 Walsh and McDowell 88.

26 Jones, "Towards A New Theatre."

27 Jones, "Towards A New Theatre."

28 Jarka Burian, *The Scenography of Josef Svoboda* (Middletown, CT: Wes-
leyan University Press, 1971) 77–91. Burian's excellent work on
Svoboda contains an equally excellent discussion of the history of
Laterna Magika and related forms in Czechoslovakia and Europe.

29 Burian 77–91.

30 Karel Koutsky, Jan Kozel, Jindrich Smetana, Josef Svoboda, "A New
Workshop for the Laterna Magika," *Interscenea*, October 1982: 52.

31 Koutsky 52.

32 Jones, *Imagination* 13.

ABOUT THE EDITOR

Delbert Unruh is currently a Professor of Theatre and Film and the Head of the Theatre Design Program at the University of Kansas. Born in 1941, in Glendive, Montana, he received his BA in Theatre at the University of Montana in 1964, and his MA in Theatre at Northwestern University in 1966.

An acknowledged authority on American and Czechoslovakian stage design theory, Professor Unruh is a Contributing Editor to *Theatre Design and Technology*, the journal of the United States Institute for Theatre Technology. In that capacity, he has written many articles on the history, relationships, and contemporary application of American and European design theory.

A member of United Scenic Artists Local 829, Professor Unruh is also a practicing professional designer in the Kansas City area. His design work has been featured in many regional, national, and international design exhibitions, most notably in the 1980 First Biennial USITT Scenography Exposition, the Czechoslovak Section of the 1987 Prague Quadriennale, and the 1990 International Exposition of Scenography in Novi Sad, Yugoslavia. He is married, has three daughters, and lives in Lawrence, Kansas.